Henrik Ibsen

A Doll's House

an English-language version by
Simon Stephens

Methuen Drama

Bloomsbury Methuen Drama

An imprint of Bloomsbury Publishing Plc

50 Bedford Square London WC1B 3DP UK

175 Fifth Avenue New York NY 10010 USA

www.bloomsbury.com

A Doll's House by Henrik Ibsen first published in this translation in 2012

British Library Cataloguing-in-Publication Data

A catalogue record for this book is available from the British Library

ISBN
PB: 978-1-4725-2641-0
ePDF: 978-1-4081-7333-6
ePub: 978-1-4081-7332-9

Typeset by Country Setting, Kingsdown, Kent CT14 8ES
Printed and bound in Great Britain

Young Vic

A Doll's House

by Henrik Ibsen

English language version by Simon Stephens

This production opened at the Young Vic on 29 June 2012 and was revived on 28 March 2013.

A DOLL'S HOUSE

by Henrik Ibsen

English language version by Simon Stephens

The Actors

Helene	**Mabel Clements**
Nils Krogstad	**Nick Fletcher**
Anna	**Leda Hodgson**
Nora Helmer	**Hattie Morahan**
Torvald Helmer	**Dominic Rowan**
Doctor Rank	**Steve Toussaint**
Kristine Linde	**Susannah Wise**
Ivar Helmer	**Vincent Curson-Smith**
	Leon Rolfe
Jon Helmer	**Nathaniel Smith**
	Jake Tuesley
Emmy Helmer	**Jowan Sonny Frankland**
	Leyna Adame Swetz
	Laszlo Corin Whitaker

The Team

Direction	**Carrie Cracknell**
Design	**Ian MacNeil**
Costumes	**Gabrielle Dalton**
Light	**Guy Hoare**
Music	**Stuart Earl**
Sound	**David McSeveney**
Choreography	**Quinny Sacks**
Casting	**Julia Horan CDG**
Hair and Make-Up Design	**Campbell Young**
Voice	**Emma Woodvine**
Assistant Director	**Sam Pritchard**
Trainee Assistant Director	**Anastasia Osei-Kuffour**
Literal Translation	**Charlotte Barslund**

In the first run at the Young Vic, Helene was played by Yolanda Kettle, Anna was played by Lynne Verrall, Ivar was played by Vincent Curson-Smith/Arthur Gledhill Franks, Jon was played by Jake Tuesley/Pip Pearce and Emmy was played by Evie Sophia Beadle-Thomas/Harry Turner/Dorothea MacGibbon.

Stage Manager	**Sarah Tryfan**
Deputy Stage Manager	**Ian Andlaw**
Assistant Stage Manager	**Lizzie Donaghy**
Costume Supervisor	**Zeb Lalljee**
Design Assistant (set)	**Jim Gaffney**
Set built by	**Miraculous Engineering,**
	Ed Wirtz, Nick Benjamin
	Rachel Mandley, Rachaelle Day,
	William Wyld
Wardrobe Assistant and Dresser	**Naimo Duale**
Wig and Hair Dressing	**Elinor McMahon**
Wardrobe Assistant	**Rosey Morling**
Costume Makers	**Pauline Parker, Debo Andrews,**
	Karen Griffths, Debs Tallentire,
	Anna Barcock
Stage Crew	**Tom Nutt**
	Georgia Pavelkovà
Sound Operator	**Amy Bramma**
Lighting Work Placement	**Isobel Howe**
Chaperones	**Valerie Joyce**
	Danielle Calvert
Violins	**Everton Nelson**
	Patrick Kiernan
Viola	**Vicci Wardman**
Cello	**Caroline Dale**
Bass	**Chris Laurence**
Flute	**Karen Jones**
Clarinet	**Nicholas Bucknall**
Harp	**Hugh Webb**

A Doll's House is generously supported by The Ulrich Family, Rita and Paul Skinner, the Young Vic Women's Group and the Royal Norwegian Embassy.

Young Vic Women's Group Rotha Bell, Marie Carli, Jane Lucas, Jill Manson, Juliet Medforth, Dounia Nadar, Midge Palley, Rita Skinner, Sandi Ulrich, Charlotte Weston.

Sam Pritchard is supported through the Jerwood Assistant Directors Programme at the Young Vic.

Anastasia Osei-Kuffour is supported through the Boris Karloff Trainee Assistant Directors Programme at the Young Vic.

Thanks to the National Theatre, Donmar Warehouse, Almeida and ETT.

BIOGRAPHIES

Henrik Ibsen

Henrik Ibsen was born in 1828 in Skien, Norway. A founder of modernism in theatre, he is one of the most influential playwrights of the 19th century. After a series of verse plays, he wrote 12 prose masterpieces. They include *The Master Builder* (1892), *Hedda Gabler* (1890), *Ghosts* (1881) and *A Doll's House* (1879). *A Doll's House* premiered at the Royal Theatre in Copenhagen, Denmark in 1879 and immediately provoked huge controversy. Even during his lifetime, *A Doll's House* was performed across the globe.

Simon Stephens

Previous plays at the Young Vic include: his adaptation of Jon Fosse's *I Am The Wind* (2011).

Other plays include: *Morning* (Traverse and Lyric Hammersmith, 2012), *Three Kingdoms* (No99/ Munich Playhouse/Lyric Hammersmith); *Trial of Ubu* (Toneelgroep Amsterdam/ Hampstead); *Wastwater* (Royal Court); *T5* (Traverse); *A Thousand Stars Explode in the Sky* (co-written with Robert Holman and David Eldridge, Lyric Hammersmith); *Marine Parade* (co-writtern with Mark Eitzel, Brighton Festival); *Punk Rock* (Lyric Hammersmith/ Royal Exchange Manchester); *Heaven* (Traverse); *Seawall* (Bush/ Traverse); *Harper Regan* (National); *Pornography* (Tricycle/ Birmingham Rep/ Edinburgh Festival/ Deutsches Schauspielhaus); *Motortown* (Royal Court); *On the Shore of the Big Wide World* (Royal Exchange Manchester/ National); *Country Music* (Royal Court); *Christmas* (Bush); *One Minute* (Crucible); *Port* (Royal Exchange Manchester); *Herons, Bluebird* (Royal Court).

Awards include: Olivier Award for Best New Play for *On the Shore of the Big Wide World*; the Pearson Award for Best Play for Port; Theater Heute's Best Foreign Language Play of the Year 2007 for *Motortown*, in 2008 for *Pornography* and in 2011 for *Wastwater* and Best Foreign Playwright of the Year 2008 and 2011; What's On Stage Best New Play Award 2012 for *The Curious Incident of the Dog in the Night-time*.

Carrie Cracknell Direction

Carrie Cracknell is Associate Director of The Young Vic. From 2007 until January 2012 she was Artistic Director of the Gate Theatre. She was nominated as Best Director in the Evening Standard Awards for her work on *A Doll's House*.

Previous Young Vic: *Elektra*.

At the Gate Theatre: *Elektra, Breathing Irregular, Hedda, Shoot/Get Treasure/ Repeat, The Sexual Neuroses of Our Parents* (all Gate Theatre), *I Am Falling* (Gate Theatre and Sadler's Wells – nominated for Southbank Show Award).

Other theatre includes: *Dolls* (National Theatre of Scotland); *Stacy* (The Tron, Glasgow); *A Mobile Thriller* (National Tour and The Harbourfront, Toronto) Winner Herald Angel Award; *Broken Road* (British Council Showcase) Winner Fringe First Award; *Death and The City* (The Tron); *The Hush* (BAC and The Ohio Theatre, New York); *Macbeth* (Djanogly Theatre, Nottingham).

Carrie trained at The University of Nottingham (History), The Royal Scottish Academy of Music and Drama (Directing) and The National Theatre Studio (Directing). In 2004 Carrie won The Bruce Millar Trust Award for directors.

Ian MacNeil Design

Previous Young Vic: *Afore Night Come*, *Tintin* (also at the Barbican and The Playhouse Theatre), *Vernon God Little*.

Theatre designs include: *An Inspector Calls* (National, West End, Broadway); *Machinal* (National); *Ariodante* (English National Opera); *Festen* (Almeida/West End); *In Basildon, A Number, Plasticine, Far Away* (Royal Court), *Via Dolorosa* (Royal Court/ Broadway/West End) for the Royal Court; *Billy Elliot The Musical* (West End, Broadway, Australia and two US tours).

Awards include: two Oliviers (*An Inspector Calls* and *Ariodante*), two Critics' Circle Awards (*Machinal* and *An Inspector Calls*), two Evening Standard Awards (*A Number/Plasticine* and *Festen*) and 2006 Olivier Award nomination for Best Set Design (*Billy Elliot*).

Gabrielle Dalton Costumes

Previous Young Vic: *Joe Turner's Come and Gone*.

Current and recent work: *La Voix Humaine, Dido and Aeneas, Joshua, Carmen* (Opera North); *Carmen* (Salzburg Easter and Summer Festivals); Associate Costume Designer on *The Ring Cycle* (Nationale Reisopera, Holland); *Carmen* (revival: Flanders Opera).

Previously: *Rusalka* (Grange Park Opera); *Magical Night, The Red Balloon* (ROH2 and tour); *The Barber of Seville* (Savoy Opera); *Three Water Plays* (Almeida Opera Festival); *Turandot* (NRO); *Le nozze di Figaro* (International tour); *Of Thee I Sing, Let 'em Eat Cake, Les Noces, Ruddigore* (Opera North).

Gabrielle will design costumes for *Fiddler on the Roof* (2015) and *Boris Godunov* (2016) for Grange Park Opera and *Fanciulla del West* (Opera North), *Don Quichotte* (2014) for GPO.

Guy Hoare Light

Previous Young Vic: *Going Dark, Elektra, The Story of an African Farm*.

Theatre includes: *NSFW, In Basildon* (Royal Court); *Be Near Me, Serenading Louie* (Donmar Warehouse); *A Delicate Balance, Waste* (Almeida); *And No More Shall We Part* (Hampstead); *Electra* (The Gate); *Peter Pan* (NTS); *Future Proof* (Traverse); *Wild Oats, Faith Healer* (Bristol Old Vic); *Macbeth* (West Yorkshire Playhouse); *Assassins* (Sheffield Theatres).

Dance includes: *The Metamorphosis* (ROH2); *Square Map of Q4* (Bonachela Dance Company); *Frontline* (Aterbaletto); *Pavlova's Dogs* (Scottish Dance Theatre); *Dream* (NDCWales); *Mischief* (Theatre Rites); *Made In Heaven* (Mark Bruce Company); *Bruise Blood* (Shobana Jeyasingh Dance Company).

Opera includes: *Jakob Lenz* (ENO); *The Cunning Little Vixen* (Brno); *Don Giovanni, Eugene Onegin* (ETO); *The Firework-Maker's Daughter* (The Opera Group).

Stuart Earl Music

Stuart has scored various feature films that have premiered at major international film festivals including *My Brother The Devil* (Berlinale, London & Sundance Film Festivals 2012); *Guinea Pigs* (Edinburgh 2012); *Babeldom* (Rotterdam International Film Festival 2012); *In Our Name* (London Film Festival 2010) and *Guilty Pleasures* (London Film Festival 2010).

Television includes: *The Entire History of You*, the third drama in the first series of Charlie Brooker's *Black Mirror* (Channel 4), written by Jesse Armstrong.

Stuart was selected as the first composer to be one of Screen International's Stars of Tomorrow 2012. He received the 2009 Skillset Trailblazer Award at Edinburgh Film Festival.

His work was most recently seen in *Mayday*, a major five-part drama for Kudos which screened on BBC1 in March.

David McSeveney Sound

David trained at the Central School of Speech and Drama completing a BA Hons. in Theatre Practice (Sound Design).

Previous Young Vic: *The Changeling, One for the Road, Victoria Station* (Print Room/ Young Vic); *The Girlfriend Experience* (Royal Court/ Young Vic/ Theatre Royal Plymouth).

Theatre includes: *A Winter's Tale* (RSC); *Constellations, Posh* (West End); *Stones in His Pockets* (Tricycle); *On The Record* (iceandfire); *Belong, Vera Vera Vera, Constellations, The Village Bike, Ingredient X, Posh, Disconnect, Cock, A Miracle, The Stone, Shades, 7 Jewish Children, Fear & Misery/War & Peace* (Royal Court); *Clybourne Park* (Royal Court/ West End); *The Tin Horizon* (Theatre 503); *Gaslight* (Old Vic); *Charley's Aunt, An Hour and a Half Late* (Theatre Royal Bath); *A Passage to India, After Mrs Rochester, Madame Bovary* (Shared Experience); *Men Should Weep,* (Oxford Stage Company); *Othello* (Southwark Playhouse).

Quinny Sacks Choreography

Previous Young Vic: *Punch & Judy* (ENO/Young Vic).

Theatre includes: *Hamlet, The Winters Tale* (RSC); *Machinal & Lady in the Dark* (National); *Mojo, Mouth to Mouth* (Royal Court); *Threepenny Opera* (Donmar Warehouse); *Kiss Me Like You Mean It* (Soho); *My Fair Lady, The Boyfriend* (British Tours); *Salad Days* (Riverside Studios).

Film and television includes: *Shakespeare In Love, Captain Corelli's Mandolin, Who Framed Roger Rabbit, The Singing Detective, Lipstick on my Collar, Troy, Restoration, Captain America.*

Opera includes: *The Voyage* (Met. N.Y.); *The Fairy Queen, Lady Macbeth of Mtensk, The Rakes Progress, Elixir of Love* (ENO); *L'Etoile, La Boheme, Playing Away* (Opera North).

Quinny was a dancer with Bejart and Ballet Rambert and founded her own Dance/Theatre company *Extreme Measures*.

Julia Horan CDG Casting

Previous Young Vic: *Wild Swans* (Young Vic/ART/ATC), *After Miss Julie, Government Inspector, My Dad's A Birdman, Joe Turner's Come And Gone, Glass Menagerie, Annie Get Your Gun, In The Red & Brown Water, The Good Soul Of Szechuan.*

Theatre includes: *Absent Friends* (Harold Pinter Theatre); *Backbeat* (Duke of York's/ Toronto); *South Downs/The Browning Version* (Harold Pinter Theatre/ Chichester Festival Theatre); *Clybourne Park* (Royal Court/Wyndhams); *Wastwater, The Heretic, Get Santa, Kin, Red Bud, Tribes, Wanderlust, Spur Of The Moment, Sucker Punch, Ingredient X* (Royal Court); *The Golden Dragon* (ATC); *Children's Children, Filumena, The Knot Of The Heart, Through A Glass Darkly, Measure For Measure, When The Rain Stops Falling, In A Dark Dark House, A Chain Play, The Homecoming* (Almeida).

Campbell Young Hair and Make-Up Design

Previous Young Vic: *Three Sisters, Wild Swans, Hamlet, Government Inspector, Annie Get Your Gun, The Good Soul of Szechuan, Vernon God Little, Six Characters Looking for an Author.*

Other theatre includes: *Ghost the Musical, Private Lives, Spider-Man, La Bête, Mary Stuart, Rock 'n' Roll, Sweeney Todd, Ghost, Betrayal, Million Dollar Quartet, The Children's Hour, La Bête, Love Never Dies, Breakfast at Tiffany's, Priscilla, Oliver, Billy Elliot, An Inspector Calls* (Broadway); *Les Misérables* (US tour).

Sam Pritchard Assistant Director

Previous Young Vic: *Fireface*

Theatre includes: *There Has Possibly Been An Incident, Galka Motalka* (Royal Exchange); *Money Matters* (nabokov/Soho); *The Parrot House* (Liverpool Everyman).

Theatre as assistant director includes: *Wozzeck* (ENO); *Paper Dolls* (Tricycle); *Comedy of Errors, 1984, Blithe Spirit, The Miser* (Royal Exchange).

Sam was the New Writing Associate at the Royal Exchange 2010-12 and is the winner of the JMK Award for Young Directors 2012.

Sam is supported through the Jerwood Assistant Directors Programme at the Young Vic.

JERWOOD CHARITABLE FOUNDATION

Anastasia Osei-Kuffour Trainee Assistant Director

Anastasia took part in the Young Vic introduction to directing course and since then has assisted on several young people's projects.

Theatre as assistant director includes: *The Wonder of the Wandle* (Morden Hall Park); *Fräulein Else* (Nursery Theatre).

Anastasia is supported through the Boris Karloff Trainee Assistant Directors Programme at the Young Vic.

Charlotte Barslund Literal Translation

Charlotte translates Scandinavian plays and novels.

Her translation of Strindberg's *The Pelican* was broadcast on BBC Radio 3. She translated Ingmar Bergman's version of *Ghosts* by Henrik Ibsen, which was performed at the Barbican. Her translation of the Norwegian crime novel *Calling Out For You!* by Karin Fossum was nominated for the 2005 Gold Dagger Award by the British Crime Writers' Association.

Other translated novels include: *Machine* and *The Brummstein* by Peter Adolphsen and *Pierced* and *Burned* by Thomas Enger.

Mabel Clements Helene

Theatre includes: *Angus Thongs and Even More Snogging* (West Yorkshire Playhouse); *Out of Me* (Soho/ NYT).

Whilst training at The Guildhall School of Music and Drama Mabel's credits include: Hattie in *Kiss Me Kate*, Iphigenia in *Iphigenia at Aulis*, *House of Atreus*, Joanna Trout in *Dear Brutus* & Cathy in *DNA*.

Film: *The Window.*

Radio: *Beware of Pity* (BBC Radio 4).

Voiceover credits include: *Sherlock Holmes, My Week with Marilyn, Skyfall, Harry Potter 4, 5* and *6* and *The Chronicles of Narnia.*

Nick Fletcher Nils Krogstad

Previous Young Vic: *The Shawl.*

Theatre includes: *The Country Wife* (Royal Exchange); *A Woman Killed With Kindness, The White Guard, The Overwhelming, Once In A Lifetime, Playing With Fire, The UN Inspector* (National); *Twisted Tales* (Lyric Hammersmith); *Dial M For Murder* (West Yorkshire Playhouse); *Thyestes* (Arcola); *A Midsummer Night's Dream, The Two Gentlemen Of Verona* (Regent's Park); *King Lear* (Old Vic); *Star Quality* (Apollo); *Love's Labours Lost* (ETT); *All's Well That Ends Well* (Chicago Shakespeare Theater); *The Way Of The World* (Orange Tree); *Henry V, A Chaste Maid In Cheapside* (Shakespeare's Globe); *Burdalane* (BAC).

Television includes: *Silk, Harley Street, Midsomer Murders, New Tricks, True Dare Kiss, After The War.*

Leda Hodgson Anna

Leda trained at LAMDA.

Theatre includes: *A Woman of No Importance* (Trinity, Tunbridge Wells); *A Lady of Letters* (Copake NY); *Talking Talking Heads* (Theatre Maketa); *Bed Among the Lentils* (Bridewell); *Audience with Murder* (Edinburgh and Jermyn St); *Backpay, The Terrible Voice of Satan* (Royal Court); *Romeo and Juliet* (London Shakespeare Group); *Gotcha, Rack Abbey, A Midsummer Night's Dream, The Man of Mode* (Cheek by Jowl); *Now Blind Yourself* (The Place).

Television includes: *Baddiel's Syndrome, Inspector Lynley, Perfect World, Hamish Macbeth, Take Three Women.*

Radio includes: *Long Time Man.*

Film includes: *Thursday, Stone Tears, Meat.*

Hattie Morahan Nora Helmer

Recent theatre includes: *The Dark Earth And The Light Sky* (Almeida); *Sixty-Six Books* (Bush); *Plenty* (Sheffield Crucible); *The Real Thing* (Old Vic); *Time and the Conways, Three More Sleepless Nights, . . . some trace of her, The Seagull, Iphigenia at Aulis* (National); *Family Reunion* (Donmar Warehouse); *The City* (Royal Court); *See How They Run* (West End); *Twelfth Night* (West Yorkshire Playhouse); *Singer* (Tricycle); *Night of the Soul, Prisoners Dilemma, Hamlet* (RSC).

Television includes: *Midsomer Murders, Eternal Law, Outnumbered, Lewis, Money, Marple: A Pocket Full of Rye, Trial and Retribution, Sense and Sensibility, Bodies, New Tricks.*

Films includes: *Nora, Having You, Summer in February, The Bank Job, The Golden Compass.*

Hattie won both the Evening Standard Theatre Award and the Critics Circle Best Actress Award for her performance as Nora in A Doll's House, and a 2007 Ian Charleson Award for her role in *The Seagull.*

Dominic Rowan Torvald Helmer

Previous Young Vic: *After Dido* (Young Vic/ENO).

Theatre includes: *Berenice* (Donmar Warehouse); *The Village Bike* (Royal Court); *Henry VIII, A New World, As You Like It* (Shakespeare's Globe); *The Misanthrope* (West End); *The Spanish Tragedy* (Arcola); *Under the Blue Sky* (West End); *Happy Now?, Dream Play, Iphigena at Aulis, Mourning Becomes Electra, Three Sisters, The Talking Cure* (National); *A Voyage Round My Father* (Donmar Warehouse); *Way to Heaven, Forty Winks* (Royal Court).

Television includes: *Restless, Henry IV, Law and Order UK* (series 5, 6, 7), *Catwalk Dogs, Baby Boom, Trial and Retribution, The Lavender List, The Family Man, Rescue Me, Lost World, Swallow.*

Steve Toussaint Dr Rank

Theatre includes: *The Riots* (Tricycle); *Macbeth, Merchant of Venice* (RSC); *Twelfth Night* (Nottingham Playhouse); *Ruined* (Almeida); *Hapgood* (Birmingham Rep & West Yorkshire Playhouse); *Flight 5065: The Traducers* (London Eye); *Fix Up* (National); *Urban Afro-Saxons* (Talawa); 20, 000 Leagues Under the Sea (Theatre Royal Stratford East); *A Servant to Two Masters* (RSC); *To Kill A Mocking Bird* (Everyman Palace); *Someone Who'll Watch Over Me* (West End).

Television includes: *Spooks, Doctors, Skins, New Tricks, CSI:Miami, My Dad's the Prime Minister, Waking the Dead, Broken News.*

Film includes: *Asylum, Prince of Persia: The Sands of Times, Broken Lines, Mutant Chronicles, Flight of Fury, Shooting Dogs, The Sin Eater, Dog Eat Dog, Circus, Macbeth, I.D.*

Susannah Wise Kristine Linde

Theatre includes: *The Holy Rosenbergs, Sanctuary, The Prime Of Miss Jean Brodie* (National); *Heartbreak House* (Chichester); *Hero, Seven Jewish Children, Where Do We Live* (Royal Court); *Rabbit* (The Old Red Lion/ Trafalgar Studios/ New York); *Featuring Loretta* (Hampstead); *Festen* (Lyric Hammersmith/ West End); *When Harry Met Sally* (Theatre Royal Haymarket); *Three Sisters* (Playhouse); *Life After George* (Duchess).

Television includes: *Derek, PhoneShop, Joe, Secret Smile, U Be Dead, Peepshow, The Time Of Your Life, The Tennant Of Wildfell Hall, The IT Crowd, Soundproof, Secret Smile, In A Land Of Plenty, Eskimo Day, Dalziel & Pascoe.*

Film includes: *An Ideal Husband, Britannic.*

Vincent Curson-Smith Ivar Helmer

Vincent Curson-Smith is 11 years old and appears as the Young Barnabas in Tim Burton's recent film *Dark Shadows*. He has appeared in ITV's *Primeval*, and in the BBC/HBO drama *Pinochet in Suburbia*, as well as some short films.

Leon Rolfe Ivar Helmer

Leon is aged 12 years old and attends Young Actors Theatre weekly, has performed in their production of *Man of Mode* and is represented by YAT Management. He is in the Post Office advertising campaign. Leon plays team football, ice-skates regularly and has won GB bronze medals for fencing. He is half German, loves languages, reading and plays piano.

Nathaniel Smith Jon Helmer

Theatre includes: Munchkin in *The Wizard of Oz* (London Palladium).

Nathaniel is 9 years old and has attended Stagecoach in Sutton for four years. He enjoys football, tennis, street dance and singing.

Jake Tuesley Jon Helmer

Theatre includes: Benjamin in *Priscillia Queen of the Desert* (West End); Sneezy in *Snow White* (Chequer Mead); *Peter Pan, Dick Whittington, Aladdin* (Chequer Mead) and *Fiddler on the Roof* (The Hawth). He has also starred in a commercial for First Choice holidays.

Jake, aged 9, loves to perform which he has been doing since he was 3. He is part of his school choir and attends dance and singing lessons.

Young Vic

Our shows
We present the widest variety of classics, new plays, forgotten works and music theatre. We tour and co-produce extensively within the UK and internationally.

Our artists
Our shows are created by some of the world's great theatre people alongside the most adventurous of the younger generation. This fusion makes the Young Vic one of the most exciting theatres in the world.

Our audience
. . . is famously the youngest and most diverse in London. We encourage those who don't think theatre is 'for them' to make it part of their lives. We give 10% of our tickets to schools and neighbours irrespective of box office demand, and keep prices low.

Our partners near at hand
Each year we engage with 10,000 local people – individuals and groups of all kinds including schools and colleges – by exploring theatre on and off stage. From time to time we invite our neighbours to appear on our stage alongside professionals.

Our partners further away
By co-producing with leading theatre, opera, and dance companies from around the world we create shows neither partner could achieve alone.

The Cut Bar and Restaurant
Our bar and restaurant is a relaxing place to meet and eat. An inspired mix of classic and original play-themed dishes made from fresh, free-range and organic ingredients creates an exciting menu.
www.thecutbar.com

The Young Vic is a company limited by guarantee, registered in England No. 1188209

VAT registration No. 236 673 348

The Young Vic (registered charity No 268876) received public funding from

Major sponsor of the Young Vic

Lead sponsor of the Young Vic's funded ticket scheme

Get more from the Young Vic online

Sign up to receive email updates at youngvic.org/register

 youngvictheatre

 @youngvictheatre

youngviclondon

youngviclondon.wordpress.com

THE YOUNG VIC COMPANY

THE YOUNG VIC

> 'The Young Vic is one of our great producing theatres.'
> *The Independent*
>
> 'The Young Vic is one of our favourite theatres, resolutely going its own way as bustling and unorthodox as ever.'
> *The Sunday Times*
>
> 'The sexiest theatre in London.' *Time Out*

To produce our sell-out, award-winning shows and provide thousands of free activities through our Taking Part programme requires major investment. Find out how you can make a difference and get involved.

As an individual . . . become a Friend, donate to a special project, attend our unique gala events or remember the Young Vic in your will.

As a company . . . take advantage of our flexible memberships, exciting sponsorship opportunities, corporate workshops, CSR engagement and venue hire.

As a trust or foundation . . . support our innovative and forward-thinking programmes on stage and off.

Are you interested in events . . . hire a space in our award-winning building and we can work with you to create truly memorable workshops, conferences or parties.

For more information visit

youngvic.org/support us

020 7922 2810

SUPPORTING THE YOUNG VIC

The Young Vic relies on the generous support of many trusts, companies, and individuals to continue our work, on and off stage. For their recent support we thank

Public Funders
Arts Council England
British Council
Lambeth Borough Council
Southwark Council

Major Supporter
Otkritie Capital

Corporate Supporters
American Airlines
Barclays
Bloomberg
Coutts
Markit
Taylor Wessing LLP
The Cooperative

Corporate Members
aka
Bates, Wells & Braithwaite
Bloomberg
Clifford Chance
Ingenious Media Plc
Lane Consulting
Memery Crystal
Promise

Partners
Eric Abraham
Tony & Gisela Bloom
Chris & Jane Lucas
Patrick McKenna
Simon and Midge Palley
Jon and Noralee Sedmak
Justin Shinebourne
Ramez and Tiziana Sousou
The Ulrich Family
Anda & Bill Winters

Soul Mates
Royce and Rotha Bell
Beatrice Bondy
Patrick Handley
Justin and Jill Manson
Miles Morland
Rita and Paul Skinner

Jane Attias
Chris & Ruth Baker
Rory Bateman
Chris & Frances Bates

The Bickertons
Katie Bradford
CJ & LM Braithwaite
Tim & Caroline Clark
Kay Ellen Consolver
Caroline & Ian Cormack
Susan Dark
Miel de Botton
Annabel Duncan-Smith
Robyn Durie
Jennifer & Jeff Eldredge
Paul Gambaccini
Annika Goodwille
Sarah Hall
Richard Hardman & Family
Jaakko Harlas
Nik Holttum & Helen Brannigan
Maxine Isaacs
Suzanne & Michael Johnson
John Kinder & Gerry Downey
Tom Keatinge
Mr & Mrs Herbert Kretzmer
Carol Lake
Jude Law
Michael Lebovitz & Ana Paludi
Ann Lewis
Tony Mackintosh
James & Sue Macmillan
Ian McKellen
John McLaughlin
Juliet Medforth
Barbara Minto
Dounia & Sherif Nadar
Georgia Oetker
Sally O'Neill
Rob & Lesley O'Rahilly
Anthony & Sally Salz
Charles & Donna Scott
Bhagat Sharma
Dasha Shenkman
Lois Sieff
Melissa A. Smith
Jan & Michael Topham
The Tracy Family
Donna & Richard Vinter
Jimmy & Carol Walker
Rob Wallace
Edgar & Judith Wallner
George & Patricia White
Mrs Fiona Williams

Trust Supporters
29th May 1961 Charitable Trust
95.8 Capital FM's Help a Capital Child
BBC Children in Need
Boris Karloff Foundation
The Boshier-Hinton Foundation
The City Bridge Trust
John S Cohen Foundation
D'Oyly Carte Charitable Trust
Equitable Charitable Trust
Esmée Fairbairn Foundation
Garfield Weston Foundation
Gatsby Charitable Foundation
Genesis Foundation
Goethe-Institut
Golden Bottle Trust
Gosling Foundation
Harold Hyam Wingate Foundation
Henry Smith Charity
Jerwood Charitable Foundation
John Ellerman Foundation
John Thaw Foundation
KPMG Foundation
Lambeth HAP
The Limbourne Trust
Martin Bowley Charitable Trust
Newcomen Collett Foundation
The Portrack Charitable Trust
Progress Foundation
Red Hill Trust
Richard Radcliffe Trust
Royal Norwegian Embassy
The Royal Victoria Hall Foundation
Santander Foundation
Sir Siegmund Warburg's Voluntary Settlement
The Steel Charitable Trust

and all other donors who wish to remain anonymous.

markit™

Markit is proud to be the Lead Sponsor of the

Young Vic's Funded Ticket Programme

Enabling theatre to be enjoyed by all

www.markit.com

A Doll's House

Characters

Nora Helmer
Torvald Helmer
Doctor Rank
Kristine Linde
Nils Krogstad
Ivar Helmer
Jon Helmer
Emmy Helmer
Anna
Helene

The play takes place in the Helmers' house in a town in Norway in 1878.

One

A living room.
Three doors. A window.
A piano. Tables. Armchairs. Sofas.
A rocking chair.
Engravings on the wall.
A whatnot holding ornaments. A bookcase.
A carpet on the floor.

The fire is lit.

It is winter. It is daytime.

A bell rings in the hall.

After a time **Nora** *enters. She is carrying an armful of parcels.* **Helene**, *the maid who opened the door for her, follows.*

Nora   Hide the Christmas tree properly, Helene. I don't want the children to see it until it's been decorated. How much is the delivery?

Helene   I think it was one seventy-five, Mrs Helmer.

Nora   Here. Give him five. Tell him to keep the change.

Helene   Very good Mrs Helmer. I will.

Nora   Is Mr Helmer at home?

Helene   I believe he's in his study.

Nora   Thank you, Helene.

Helene   Not at all.

She exits. **Nora** *stands. She smiles. She hums a little. She goes to take her coat off. She stops. She finds a bag of chocolates in her pocket. She takes out the bag. She starts eating the chocolates.*

Torvald *calls from his study.*

Torvald   Is that a little swallow out there?

Nora   It might be.

Torvald   Can I hear a chaffinch fluttering around my house?

Nora   You might be able to.

Torvald   When did you get home?

Nora   Just this second.

She finishes the chocolates. She licks her fingers clean. She puts the bag back in her coat pocket, takes the coat off and hangs it up.

Torvald, come and see what I bought.

After a brief time one of the doors opens and **Torvald Helmer** *stands in the doorway.*

Torvald   I'm trying to work in here.

Nora   I know. I'm sorry.

Torvald   Has my little hamster been spending all of my money again?

Nora   Not all of it.

Torvald   Did you buy all this?

Nora   Is that very bad?

Torvald   It's a little bit bad. Not terribly bad.

Nora   But we can afford it, this year, can't we?

He looks at her as he comes into the room to examine her purchases.

With the salary you're going to get? And the lots and lots of money you're going to earn? This is the first Christmas when we haven't had to count every penny.

He struggles to take his eyes off her. She enjoys him watching her.

Torvald   I won't actually get paid anything for another three months.

She stands in front of him. She smiles up at him.

Nora   Well, we're just going to have to borrow money until then aren't we?

Torvald   Nora.

She kisses him. He checks the maids are not within earshot and kisses her back.

You're like a little girl.

He kisses her some more. Stands away. Smiles.

What would you do if I borrowed three months' salary today and you spent every last bit of it during the Christmas holiday and then a tile fell off our roof and landed on my head on New Year's Eve and killed me stone dead?

Nora   That's horrible.

Torvald   It could happen though. What would you do?

Nora   If that happened, the last people I would be worried about would be the strangers I owed money to.

Torvald   I'm being serious.

Nora   So am I.

He kisses her.

Torvald   You know what I think about borrowing money.

Nora   I do.

He kisses her again.

Torvald   We've done so well until now.

Nora   I know.

He kisses her again.

Torvald   We can hold our breath for a few more months.

She smiles at him and heads away.

Are you cross with me?

Nora   No.

Torvald   Are you sulking? Are you hiding your head in your wings?

He takes his wallet out. He takes forty crowns from it. He goes up behind her.

I wonder if you can guess what I've got behind my back.

She turns quickly.

Nora   Is it money?

He gives her the money he took out from his wallet.

Torvald   I do understand, you know, how expensive Christmas can be.

She counts the money he's given her.

Nora   Thank you. Thank you. Thank you. I promise you I'll make it last.

Torvald   You really better had.

Nora   I will. I swear.

She kisses him. Then breaks away.

But you didn't see what I bought. Come here. Have a look. I got some new clothes for Ivar. They were from the last season so they were really rather cheap. Don't tell him. He won't notice. And look. I got him a sword. *En garde!*

She draws the sword like a musketeer. He smiles at her.

It's not real. Don't panic.

Torvald   I wasn't panicking.

Nora   I got a horse and a trumpet for Jon.

Torvald   A trumpet?

She blows into it. She passes it to him. He tries blowing into it. Can't make a noise.

Nora   And look at this. I got Emmy a house for her dolls. It's rather little. But she's only going to break it anyway. I got some fabric and scarves for Helene and Anna. Anna should have more than Helene, really.

Torvald *approaches an unopened box on a table.*

Torvald   And what's in that box?

She blocks his path.

Nora   Don't touch that! You're not allowed to see that until tonight. Do you promise me?

He kisses her. She kisses him back.

Torvald   And has my little skylark thought about what she'd like to find in her nest?

Nora   I don't need anything.

Torvald   Yes, you do. Tell me what you'd like.

Nora   I can't think.

Torvald   Try. Tell me anything. As long as it's not completely unreasonable.

Nora   Well, there is one thing.

Torvald   And what's that?

She plays with a button on his shirt without looking at him.

Nora   If you really, really wanted to get me something, I mean.

Torvald   What?

Nora   Do you promise that you won't be cross with me?

Torvald   Nora, you are insufferable.

Nora   You could give me some money.

Torvald   Money?

Nora   Only as much as you think you can spare.

He looks at her.

And then when I find something I like I can buy it for myself but I'll know that the money came from you.

Torvald   No.

Nora   I could wrap the money in beautiful golden paper and hang it on the Christmas tree. Wouldn't that be fun?

Torvald   It would be a very strange type of fun, Nora.

Nora   It's actually quite sensible when you think about it. It'll give me time to think about what I really want most.

Torvald   Nora, I know you.

Nora   I know you do.

Torvald   You'll take all the money and you'll spend it all on the house or you'll waste it on things that are entirely unnecessary and not leave anything for yourself at all.

Nora   I won't, I promise.

Torvald   Do you know what the defining characteristic of the swallow is?

Nora *looks at him.*

Torvald   It looks very, very sweet. It flies terribly high. But it really is extraordinarily expensive to keep the thing shining so very brightly.

Nora   I'm not entirely sure that birds do actually shine, Torvald.

Torvald   You know what I'm talking about.

Nora   I try my hardest to save everything I can.

Torvald   I know you do. I know you try. You just don't always succeed.

Nora   Well, if you knew the expenses that we swallows have to deal with, Torvald.

Torvald   You are a strange little creature, aren't you? You're like your father. You try so many different ways to get your hands on money and then once you've got it, it just runs like dust between your fingers.

Nora   I wish I were more like my father sometimes.

He looks at her.

Torvald   You don't need to be more like anybody. I wouldn't change the slightest part of you. Not for anything in the world. But wait. Hold on just a second. I've noticed something about you.

Nora   What?

Torvald   Something in your eye.

Nora   What?

Torvald   You look so – so – how should I put it?

Nora   What?

Torvald   Devious all of a sudden?

Nora   Devious?

Torvald   Yes. Devious. Here. Look at me.

He kisses her.

I knew it.

Nora   What?

Torvald   I think somebody has been eating chocolates again.

Nora   Not me.

Torvald   Somebody couldn't resist going past a certain bakery –

Nora   It wasn't me Torvald, I swear.

Torvald   Somebody has been nibbling on a nobble of butter.

Nora   I haven't. What's a 'nobble'?

Torvald   Somebody's dipped their beak into a little bag of macaroons.

Nora   Macaroons?! Torvald, I promised. I'd never break a promise I made to you.

Torvald   I'm joking. Calm down.

Don't worry.

I believe you.

They look at each other.
They smile.

Nora   Did you remember to invite Jens for dinner this evening?

Torvald   I'll ask him this morning.

Nora   Do.

Torvald   He doesn't really need asking anyway. He knows he dines with us. It goes without saying.

I'm rather excited about tonight.

Nora   I am too.

Torvald   I did take the liberty of ordering one or two rather decent bottles of wine, I'm afraid.

Nora   Or three. Or four.

He smiles at her.

Nora   The children are beside themselves with excitement.

Torvald   It makes such a difference, you know?

Nora   What does?

Torvald   Securing my position.

Nora   It's just wonderful.

Torvald   Do you remember last Christmas? It's an improvement on that, I think.

Nora   Of course it is.

Torvald   You spent three weeks locked away every night until way after midnight making – what was it?

Nora   Flowers.

Torvald   That's right, flowers for the Christmas tree. And then the cat got in and tore every last one of them to pieces.

Nora   That wasn't my fault.

Torvald   I hardly saw you for weeks. I've never been so bored in all my life.

He goes to her.

Nora   I wasn't bored at all.

Torvald   Now I don't have to sit here on my own being bored and you don't have to torture your beautiful, sparkling eyes.

He kisses her eyes. She lets him.

And your delicate, fine, little hands.

He kisses her hands. She lets him.
The bell rings in the hall. He pauses in his kissing. Then kisses her neck.

Nora   Torvald.

He doesn't stop.

Torvald, please. Someone's here.

Torvald   We can ignore them.

Nora   We can't.

Torvald   We can pretend we're not at home.

Nora   Helene will answer the door.

Torvald   It'll be Dr Rank. He'll go directly to my room. She can entertain him with stories of her scandalous employers.

Nora   Torvald. I'm being serious.

He looks at her.

Torvald   So am I.

He smiles. She smiles back.
Helene *enters.*

Torvald   Was it Dr Rank, Helene?

Helene   Yes it was, sir.

Torvald   And did he go directly to my room?

Helene   Yes he did, sir.

Torvald   Thank you, Helene.

He exits into his study. He winks at **Nora** *as he leaves.* **Nora** *smiles as she watches him go.*

Nora   Thank you, Helene.

Helene   Mrs Helmer. There is a lady here. A stranger.

Nora   A stranger? Good Lord, how exciting!

Helene *is slightly thrown by* **Nora**'s *tone and doesn't completely know how to respond.*

Helene   Should I show her in, madam?

Nora   Straight away.

Helene   Very good.

Helene *exits.* **Nora** *is left alone for a few moments.*
She thinks.
She is distracted when **Kristine Linde** *enters.* **Kristine** *catches* **Nora** *by surprise.*

Kristine   Hello, Nora.

Nora *turns and looks at her for moment.*

Nora   Hello.

Kristine   You don't recognise me, do you?

Nora   I'm not sure. Have we – I'm so sorry.

Kristine   It's Kristine.

Nora   Kristine! How could I not recognise you? I'm so sorry.

Kristine   It has been ten years, Nora.

Nora   It hasn't? Oh my Lord, it has. Ten years. Have you come all this way in this weather?

Kristine   I arrived this morning on the steamer.

Nora   The steamer? At Christmas time. Good God you're brave. How lovely. Here. Take your coat off. You're freezing. Here. Sit here. No, you sit in the armchair. I'll sit here.

She sits **Kristine** *by the armchair and sits on the rocking chair. She holds* **Kristine**'s *hands and gazes at her.*

Nora   Look at you. How could I not recognise you? Look at your skin. You've lost weight, it must be that.

Kristine   I've got old.

Nora   We've both got a little bit older, Kristine. Not much older we haven't.

She gazes at **Kristine**.

Listen to me. Chattering away. I'm so sorry.

Kristine   What for?

Nora   Kristine, I heard about your husband.

Kristine   Did you?

Nora   I feel so ashamed.

Kristine   Why?

Nora   I meant to write to you. I honestly did. I kept putting it off. Something always got in the way.

Kristine   That's all right.

Nora   And then it just felt too late.

Kristine   Nora, please don't. I understand.

Nora   It was horrible of me.

Kristine   It wasn't.

Nora   You went through so much.

Kristine   It was three years ago.

Nora   You didn't have any children?

Kristine   No.

Nora   And is it true that he really didn't leave you anything?

Kristine   Not even grief or a sense of loss to nurture.

Nora *looks at her.*

Kristine   It happens sometimes.

She smiles at **Nora** *and strokes her hair.*

Nora   It must be so hard for you.

I've got three children. They're out with their nanny.

Kristine, please. Tell me everything. Tell me everything about yourself. Tell me everything that's happened to you. Tell me everything you've done. I promise you today I'll only pay attention to you and not talk about myself at all. Apart from telling you one thing.

Kristine   What's that?

Nora   Did you hear?

Kristine   Hear what?

Nora   Torvald has been made the manager of the Savings Bank.

Kristine   Torvald?

Nora   My husband.

Kristine   Nora!

Nora   I know. He's been working as a lawyer for all the time that I've known him. But the law is so unstable as a career path. Especially if you commit to only taking cases that you really, truly believe in. And Torvald never wanted to do anything else. He starts at the bank in the New Year. He gets such an increase in his salary and he gets dividends on top of what he earns. It's going to change everything for us. We can live exactly as we've always wanted to. You've no idea how relieved I feel. You've no idea how much money he's going to make.

Kristine   Nora, you haven't changed at all, have you?

Nora   What do you mean?

Kristine   I remember in school you were so excited by just the idea of spending money.

Nora   Torvald says I still am. But it's not always been easy, Kristine. We've had a difficult few years. We've had to work so hard.

Kristine   Both of you?

Nora   Yes, both of us. I took in needlework. I did some crocheting and embroidery. I did all kinds of things. Straight after we married Torvald started working for himself. He had to; just to be able to make the money that we needed, because there was no way he was going to get any sort of promotion in the place he was working when I met him. He took on so much work, Kristine, you wouldn't believe. He worked from the start of the morning to the middle of the night. He worked far too hard if the truth were told. He worked so hard that it got to a point that he became quite ill. He had to go to a doctor. They told us he should rest. They told us we should head south. We went to Italy.

Kristine   To Italy?

Nora   Yes. We spent a whole year there. It wasn't easy, Kristine. It was just after Ivar was born. He was so little to travel. But we had no choice. It was the most wonderful time. I honestly believe that it saved Torvald's life. It did cost an awful lot of money.

Kristine   I can imagine.

Nora   Nine and a half thousand.

Kristine *looks at her.*

Nora   Are you very shocked?

Kristine   Not shocked. It's just lucky you were able to –

Nora   We got the money from my father.

Kristine   I see.

Nora It was awful because he was so ill too. At the same time. He was dying, Kristine. Can you imagine how it felt to not be able to spend time with him and to not be able to go and nurse him?

Kristine You were so fond of him.

Nora I was here. It was just before Ivar was born. I couldn't travel anywhere. And Torvald was so ill. My father! I never saw him again. It was the hardest thing that's ever happened to me.

We left a month later. Torvald came back cured.

A brief pause. **Kristine** *examines* **Nora**.

Kristine Nora, wasn't the gentleman on the stairs . . . ?

Nora The gentleman?

Kristine As I arrived. A gentleman passed me on the stairs. I thought the maid said he was a doctor.

Nora Oh that's Jens. Dr Rank. He's not a doctor. Well, he is. But he's not coming here as a doctor. He's our closest friend. He comes to see us every day. Torvald hasn't had a single day's illness since we got back from Italy. And the children are well and healthy and happy and so am I. Oh, but this is terrible. I'm being awful. I'm talking on and on about myself.

She sits at **Kristine***'s feet and rests her arms on her knees.*

Nora Don't be cross with me.

Kristine I'm not.

Nora Kristine, is it really true that you didn't love your husband?

Kristine *smiles at* **Nora**.

Kristine That is true, yes.

Nora Why did you marry him then?

Kristine My mother was ill. She couldn't leave the house. She couldn't get out of bed. She couldn't do anything. I had to look after my two little brothers. He asked me. I didn't think it was fair to anybody to say no.

Nora   Was he very rich?

Kristine   I think he was, yes. But when he died his business completely collapsed. There was nothing left of it at all.

Nora   What did you do?

Kristine   I did anything I could think of. I got a job managing a shop for a while. I got a job in a school. All I've done for the past three years is work. And then a short while ago my mother died. And my brothers have got positions of their own. They don't need me any more.

Nora   You must feel so relieved.

Kristine   I feel empty. It's like I have no one to live for any more.

Nora *gets up.*

Kristine   I couldn't stand being at home. The place started to feel so horribly remote. I thought it would be easier to find work here. I need work that will challenge me. I need something that can make me think.

Nora   Oh Kristine. Are you sure? You look so tired. You'd be so much better taking some rest. You'd be so much better heading to the South.

Kristine   I don't have a father who can pay for me to do that.

A beat.

Nora   Please don't be angry with me.

Kristine   No. I'm sorry. Please don't you be angry with me. That's the worst thing about having nothing to do. When you've nobody to work for you spend all your time thinking about yourself. Your mind turns bitter. You won't believe this, but when you told me about your husband's new position I was beside myself with happiness not because of what it meant for you but because of what it might mean for me.

Nora   Do you think he might be able to help you?

Kristine *looks at* **Nora**. *Says nothing*. **Nora** *smiles*.

Nora   He will. Just leave it to me. I know exactly how to get my own way with him. I'll place the idea in his mind.

Kristine   Nora.

Nora   Don't thank me. I so want to help you.

Kristine   You have no idea how difficult my life has been.

Nora   Don't I?

Kristine   You're still so much of a child.

Nora   Is that what you think?

Everybody says that about me. They've no idea. If I told you some of the things that I've had to deal with in my life.

Kristine   I'm not talking about your needlework.

Nora   People shouldn't underestimate me, Kristine. You shouldn't underestimate me.

Kristine *looks at* **Nora**.

Kristine   I don't underestimate anybody.

Nora   You must be very proud that you worked so hard for your mother.

Kristine   I am.

Nora   You must be very proud of everything you did for your brothers.

Kristine   I don't think there's anything wrong about that.

Nora   Well, if you knew what I had to be proud of then you wouldn't think I was so much of a child.

Kristine   What are you talking about?

Nora   Keep your voice down. If Torvald heard – He must never know, Kristine. Nobody must ever know.

Kristine   Know what?

Nora   Come here.

She brings **Kristine** *to whisper to her.*

Nora   It was me.

Kristine   What was you?

Nora   I saved Torvald's life.

Kristine   What do you mean, you saved his life?

Nora   If Torvald hadn't gone to Italy he would never have survived.

Kristine   You said that.

Nora   My father didn't give us a penny. I found all the money on my own.

Nobody knows. Everybody thinks it was my father. It wasn't. It was me.

Kristine   How could you possibly do that? Did you win the lottery?

Nora   The lottery? Where's the skill in winning the lottery?

Kristine   Well, where did you get ten thousa – ?

Nora *smiles at her. She hums a little tune.*

Kristine   You couldn't borrow it.

Nora   Why not?

Kristine   Not without your husband's consent?

Nora   Couldn't I? All you need is a little business sense. All you need is to be a bit clever.

Kristine   'A bit clever'?

Nora   Maybe I didn't borrow it. There are other ways to find money, Kristine. Maybe I was given it by one of my admirers. When a woman is as attractive as I am, Kristine, you'll find they have themselves rather a lot of –

Kristine   You're mad.

Nora   You really want to know now, don't you?

Kristine   Nora, have you done something foolish?

Nora   Is it foolish to save your husband's life?

Kristine, he wasn't allowed to know anything. He wasn't even allowed to know just how ill he really was. The doctors spoke to me, not him. They told me his life was in danger. They told me that the only thing that could save him was a trip away from the darkness and the cold here and down into the South. I had to discover a way of persuading him to leave without him ever knowing how ill he was. I told him how jealous I was of all the other wives who travelled abroad with their husbands. It was his job to look after me. I cried. I begged. He had to indulge me. I suggested he borrow some money. He got so angry. He told me that his only real duty as a husband was not to give in to my little whims and moods. But I needed to save him. I needed to find another way.

Kristine   Did your father never –

Nora   He died before he ever knew.

Kristine   And you've never admitted anything to Torvald?

Nora   How could I? He would be so embarrassed. He would be humiliated.

Kristine *looks at* **Nora**.

Some time.

Kristine   Will you ever tell him, do you think?

Nora   Oh, maybe one day. When I'm old. And tired and haggard. When I'm not quite as beautiful as I am now. I'm being serious. When he's stopped enjoying watching me dance for him. And dressing for him. When he no longer cares about my little performances for him. It would be a good thing to have a little secret up my sleeve.

What am I talking about? That'll never happen.

Kristine *looks at* **Nora** *for a while.*

Well? What do you think? Do you still think I'm a little helpless child?

Kristine   I don't know what to think.

Nora   It's not been easy I have to admit. There's something in the business world called quarterly interest. And there's something else in the business world, which is known as repayment. It can really be so terribly difficult to get hold of. I've had to save wherever I could. I couldn't take anything from the housekeeping because Torvald had to live well. I couldn't let the children become badly dressed. Every penny he gave me for the children I spent on making their lives as happy as I possibly could. Each time Torvald gave me money for new dresses or for things like that or for anything really I saved half of it and bought the simplest, cheapest materials I could find. He never noticed. It's just a good thing that everything looks so good on me.

But it was hard. It's so important to be finely dressed, Kristine, don't you think?

Last winter I managed to get a job copying. I locked myself in my room and sat and wrote every evening until the middle of the night. I got so tired. But do you know I rather enjoyed myself. Sitting there. Earning money. It was like being a man.

Kristine   Nora, how much of the money have you been able to pay off?

Nora   I'm not really entirely sure. It can be terribly difficult to stay on top of everything a lot of the time. All I know is that I've paid everything I managed to scrape together. Sometimes I haven't known at all what I was going to do. Sometimes I did wonder what it would be like if a fine, rich gentleman fell in love with me.

Kristine   A gentleman?

Nora   A gentleman in my head. And this gentleman, in my head, he died and they opened his will and it said in big black letters, 'All of my money and everything I own must be paid out and given to the miraculous Mrs Nora Helmer with immediate effect. In cash.'

Kristine   Nora, who are you talking about? Who is this gentleman?

Nora   He's nobody. He never existed. He was just somebody I made up. But it doesn't matter any more. That boring old fart can get out of my head now. I don't need to worry about him or his will any more. I'm free.

She leaps to her feet and claps her hands.

I'm free to do anything I want to do. To play with my children all day if I want to. To stroll around a beautiful and neat and elegant home. To have everything exactly the way that Torvald likes it. And soon spring will be here. And the skies will be big and blue. And maybe we can travel again. Maybe I'll get to see that sea again. I feel so alive.

The bell goes in the hall.

Kristine   You've got more visitors. I should leave.

Nora   No. Don't. Stay. I'm not expecting anybody. It'll be somebody for Torvald.

Helene *comes to the doorway. She looks in and examines the room a touch before she speaks.*

Helene   I'm so sorry, Madam. A gentleman is here who wants to talk to Mr Helmer. But I didn't know what to do because Dr Rank is still in there with Mr Helmer and I didn't know if I should disturb them or ask the gentleman to wait and if I did I didn't know where to send him to. To wait.

Nora   Who is he, Helene?

Krogstad *calls from the hallway outside.*

Krogstad   It's just me, Mrs Helmer.

Nora   Thank you. I'll deal with the gentleman.

Helene   Very good.

She goes. **Krogstad** *comes to the doorway from the hallway.*
Kristine *turns towards the window away from the room.*

Nora   What do you want to talk to my husband about?

Krogstad   Oh. Just bank business. I have a small position in
the Savings Bank and now that your husband is to be our
manager –

Nora   Are you lying to me?

Krogstad   No. I'm not. Why would I lie about something
like that?

Nora   Well. Could you please wait outside the door to the
study? You can wait in the hallway. He won't be long, I'm sure.

She turns away from him. He leaves to wait for **Helmer**. **Nora**
closes the door to the hallway behind him. **Kristine** *turns to her.*
Nora *turns away.*

Kristine   Nora. Who was that man?

Nora   Oh. He's a lawyer.

Kristine   What's his name?

Nora   Mr Krogstad.

Kristine   I thought it was him.

Nora *looks at her.*

Kristine   I knew him. A few years ago. He was our local
solicitor's clerk.

Nora   Of course.

Kristine   He's changed.

Nora   His wife died. His marriage was very unhappy, I think.
He's been left alone with their children.

Kristine   And he's working in Torvald's bank?

Nora   It would seem so.

Kristine   He's not working as a clerk any more.

Nora   I really have no idea. I don't really want to talk about his work. It's far too boring.

Dr Rank *enters from* **Torvald**'*s study.*

Rank   Oh, I'm so sorry. I'm disturbing you.

Nora   You're not. You couldn't ever disturb me. Don't be silly. Dr Rank, this is my friend Kristine Linde. Kristine, this is Dr Jens Rank.

Rank   Ah! A name I've heard spoken an awful lot in this household. Did I pass you on the stairwell when I came up the stairs?

Kristine   I think you did. I find stairs rather difficult at the moment.

Rank   Are you not well?

Kristine   I'm just tired.

Rank   And you've decided that the best thing for tiredness is to spend your days walking round town paying visits on your friends?

Kristine   I'm looking for work.

Rank   Another excellent cure for debilitating exhaustion.

Kristine   I need to live, Dr Rank.

Rank   Yes. People nowadays seem to continue to labour under the misapprehension that that remains in some way necessary.

Nora   Well, Dr Rank, I'm sure that you're rather keen on the idea of living yourself.

Rank   Oh yes, I am. Regardless of how miserable I become I still feel the need to carry on being tormented for as long a time as I can possibly get away with. All my patients feel the same way, you know? The morally sick are just as bad. We all are! There is a deeply morally sick patient in with Torvald as we speak.

Nora   Who might that be?

Rank   A man by the name of Krogstad. A lawyer. Rotten to his core. But even he began his meeting with a lengthy diatribe on the enormous importance of his continued existence.

Nora   What did he want to talk to Torvald about?

Rank   I have absolutely no idea. He was wittering on about the Savings Bank. He appears to have what he described as a 'position' down there. I don't know, Mrs Linde, if they have people like Krogstad where you come from. It's as though morally they are decaying. Yet they spend their days rushing around breathlessly sniffing out decay in others. They get their teeth into this decay. And they never let go. The morally healthy, like the physically healthy, are somewhat ignored.

Kristine   Surely it's not a bad thing to take care of the physically sick, Dr Rank?

Rank   Of course it's not. I'm just left with the sense sometimes that our entire society is turning into something of a hospital.

Nora *laughs.*

Rank   Don't laugh. I'm being serious.

Nora   I'm sure. I was laughing at something completely different. I was getting bored with what you were saying and my mind drifted off to something funny. You must tell me, Dr Rank. Are all of the people who work at the Savings Bank so dependent on Torvald?

Rank   Is that your idea of something funny?

Nora *smiles and starts humming a little.*

Nora   Oh, don't you worry about that. Don't you worry about that.

She starts to pace about the room.

I just find it rather entertaining to think about all the people that Torvald has power over.

She takes the packet of chocolates out of her pocket.

Dr Rank. Would you like a chocolate?

Rank   Chocolates! My goodness. I thought chocolates were banned in this house.

Nora   Kristine brought them for me. She didn't realise.

Kristine   I – What?

Nora   Don't panic. I won't tell Torvald. He's banned me from having chocolates. Can you believe it? He says it's because he's terrified they'll rot my teeth. I think he's far more worried about my figure. But it doesn't matter, just this once, does it, Dr Rank? Here.

She puts a chocolate in his mouth.

And one for you.

She puts a chocolate in **Kristine***'s mouth.*

Nora   And one for me. There. That's better.

Sometimes I have the most terrible urges.

Rank   Urges?

Nora   There's something, for example, that I have the most terrible urge to say right in front of Torvald.

Rank   And why can't you?

Nora   Because it's far too ugly.

Kristine   Ugly?

Rank   Well if it's ugly you're probably wise to avoid saying it in front of Torvald. He has a delicate sensibility at the best of times. But you can say it in front of us. Can't she, Mrs Linde?

Nora   I have a terrible urge to go right up to him and whisper in his ear: 'Bloody hell!'

Rank   The woman has gone quite mad!

Kristine   Nora!

Rank   Quick. He's coming. I can hear him. I think you should say it, don't you, Mrs Linde?

Nora   Shh.

She hides the bag of chocolates. **Torvald** *enters with his overcoat over his arm and his hat in his hand.*

Torvald   What's going on in here?

Nora   Nothing.

Rank   Nothing at all.

Torvald   You're all looking incredibly guilty.

Rank   It was nothing, I assure you.

Nora   Did you manage to get rid of your visitor?

Torvald   Oh yes. He's gone now.

Nora   Torvald, I forgot. You've not met. This is my dear friend Kristine Linde. She arrived in town this morning.

Torvald   Mrs Linde? I'm so sorry. It's terribly rude of me. I'm not entirely sure –

Kristine   I'm a childhood friend of your wife's. We've known each other since we were quite small.

Nora   Torvald, she has made the most remarkable journey here and all to speak to you.

Torvald   To me?

Kristine   Well, that's not entirely –

Nora   Kristine, you see, is a brilliant office worker. She has a great need to come under the direction of a deeply clever man and learn even more than she already knows.

Torvald   How very sensible.

Nora   And then she heard that you had become the manager of a bank. The news made it all the way home, Torvald, can you imagine? And as soon as she heard she came here as quickly as she could. Please. Torvald. Do you think you could find something for Kristine? She is so very dear to me.

Torvald   Are you not married, Mrs Linde?

Kristine   I am widowed.

Torvald   And you have a certain amount of experience in office work?

Kristine   A great deal of experience.

Torvald   Well. You arrived at a rather opportune moment, Mrs Linde. Let me look into it.

Kristine   Thank you.

Torvald *puts his coat on.*

Torvald   You don't need to thank me, Mrs Linde. You do, however, need to excuse me.

Rank   Wait. Torvald. I'll walk out with you.

He fetches his fur coat from the hall.

Nora   Oh Torvald, don't stay out for too long.

Torvald   An hour, Nora. No more. I promise you.

Kristine *moves to get her coat and put it on.*

Nora   Kristine. Not you as well.

Kristine   My dear Nora, I'm afraid I need to start looking for somewhere to live.

Torvald   Perhaps we could walk some of the way together, Mrs Linde.

Kristine   Thank you. I'd like that.

Torvald   I'll wait for you in the hall.

He leaves. **Nora** *helps her put her coat on.*

Nora   It's so boring that we have to live in such a tiny cramped little apartment. I wish you could stay with us here.

Kristine   Nora. Really.

Nora   It just wouldn't be possible.

Kristine   What are you thinking?

Nora   I know. I'm sorry. It's just been so good to see you.

Kristine   And it's been lovely to see you too. Thank you Nora. For everything you've done for me.

Nora   You must come back this evening.

Kristine   This evening?

Nora   I insist. And you too, Dr Rank. You are coming, aren't you?

Rank   I dare say I'll drag myself here.

Nora   Well, only if you're not too terribly ill?

Rank   I'll wrap up warm. I'm sure I'll be able to bear it.

Nora   Do.

Rank   Goodbye Nora.

He leaves.

Nora   Do come.

Kristine   I will.

Nora   I'm so happy. To see you and that you're here and that Torvald will find you work and that you're coming back this evening and for everything.

Kristine   Nora.

Nora   I know. I'm so sorry. I'm being silly. I'll stop. My dear Kristine.

Kristine   My dear, silly Nora.

She leaves.
Nora *is left alone for a while. She eats the rest of her chocolates. There is a noise off. The children and* **Anna** *have arrived home.*
Jon*, eight, runs in with his coat on.*

Jon   Mummy!

Nora   Sweetheart!

She goes to him.

Anna (*off*)　Jon. Coat. Come and take your coat off.

Jon　Sorry. Coming.

Nora　Hurry back.

Jon　I will.

He leaves.
Nora *is alone again for a short time.*
Ivar *enters. He is nine.*

Ivar　Mummy, I pulled both Emmy and Jon on the same sledge at the same time.

Nora　You didn't!

Ivar　I did.

Nora　You're so strong.

Ivar　And then I threw snowballs at them and I got Jon right in the face. But it was an accident.

Jon *enters.*

Jon　It wasn't.

Ivar　I did say sorry.

Jon　Only because Anna made you.

Nora　Oh, look at you. Your cheeks are so red. They look like apples and roses.

Ivar　Roses?!

Anna *enters holding* **Emmy**, *who is a year old.*

Nora　Red roses.

Ivar　My cheeks don't look like flowers.

Nora　Here. Let me take her. Beautiful little poppet.

She takes **Emmy** *from* **Anna** *and dances with her.*

Jon　Can I dance with you too, Mummy?

Nora　Of course you can.

The three dance together. **Nora** *sings a tune.*

Anna   Should I take her?

Nora   No. I can keep her. Please let me.

Anna   She's very tired. She rather needs a sleep.

Nora   Does she?

Anna   She's not slept all morning.

Nora   Hasn't she? Oh, very well. Why don't you take her into the nursery and you can get yourself warmed up. I want to play with my boys.

Jon   Mummy, I got chased.

Nora   Chased?

Jon   By a huge dog.

Ivar   It wasn't that huge.

Jon   It was. It was like a wolf.

Ivar   It wasn't a wolf.

Jon   It was scary.

Nora   It sounds it.

Ivar   I wasn't scared. I'm not scared of dogs.

Nora   Not even big dogs?

Ivar   No.

Nora   Not even big mummy-dogs that chase and jump and tickle!

Ivar   Ahh!!

The boys run off.
Nora *chases them.*
She catches them.
She tickles them till they tumble on the floor.

Jon   I bet if I hide you can't find me.

Ivar   I bet I could.

Jon   I didn't say you, I said Mummy.

Ivar   You're rubbish at hiding.

Nora   Ivar.

Jon   Do you think you could, Mummy?

Nora   I bet I could. I bet I could find both of you.

Ivar   You couldn't.

Nora   I could.

Ivar   You don't know the places I know.

Nora   I do, you know.

Jon   Count to twenty.

Nora   Twenty?!

Jon   Ten then.

Nora   OK, I'll count to ten.

Ivar   And close your eyes.

Nora   I always close my eyes.

Ivar   I know where I'm going.

Jon   Me too.

Ivar   You better not follow me.

Nora   Are you two ready?

Ivar *and* **Jon**   Yes, quick!

They run out. She closes her eyes and counts to ten.
Krogstad *enters and watches her as she counts.*

Nora   1, 2, 3, 4, 5, 6, 7, 8, 9, 10. Coming ready or not.

She opens her eyes to see him watching her.

Krogstad   I'm so sorry, Mrs Helmer. Do forgive me for intruding.

Nora   What do you want?

Krogstad   The front door was left wide open. People can be so careless sometimes.

Nora   My husband's not at home, Mr Krogstad.

Krogstad   No. I know that.

Nora   Then what are you doing here?

Krogstad   I wanted to talk to you.

Nora *looks at him. She goes to her door.*

Nora   Anna.

Anna *comes to the door holding* **Emmy***, who is sleeping.*

Nora   Anna, could you go and play hide-and-seek with the boys? Mr Krogstad here needs to talk to me about a matter concerning his work.

Anna   I see. Is everything all right?

Nora   Perfectly, Anna, thank you. I'm afraid the boys are hiding already. They'll have had something of a head start.

Anna   I'll find them. They always hide in the same places.

Nora   Is Emmy asleep?

Anna   Flat out.

She leaves.

Nora   It's not the first of the month for another week.

Krogstad   No. It's Christmas Eve. Imagine.

Nora   I can't possibly –

Krogstad   You don't need to. I've not come here for that. I was outside the bakery on the corner just now. I saw your husband heading into town.

Nora   Yes.

Krogstad   With a lady.

Nora *looks at him.*

Krogstad   Who was she?

Nora   Why is that any of your business?

Krogstad   Was it Kristine Linde?

Nora *says nothing.*

Krogstad   When did she get here?

Nora *says nothing.*

Krogstad   Is she a friend of yours?

Nora   I don't see what any –

Krogstad   I knew her once.

Nora   I heard.

Krogstad   I thought you would have done. What was she talking to your husband about?

Nora   Really, Mr Krogstad I refuse –

Krogstad   They were talking terribly seriously. What was he saying to her?

Nora   He's offered her a job in his bank.

A pause.

Krogstad   Was that your doing?

Nora   If my husband knew one of his employees was talking to me in this tone of voice –

Krogstad   Was that your doing, Mrs Helmer? Did you get Kristine Linde a job working for your husband?

Nora   Is that so very surprising?

Krogstad   No. No. No. No. Not at all. Not in any way.

Mrs Helmer. You need to use your influence for my benefit, now.

She looks at him.

You found Mrs Linde her job. Now you need to make sure I keep mine.

Nora   What do you mean 'keep' your job? Who's taking –

Krogstad   Don't you play the innocent with me. Do you think I don't know what you were planning? How very convenient to get me out of her way and out of your way and out of his way and to get a nice little position for your dear old school friend at the same time.

Nora   I assure you, Mr Krogstad –

Krogstad   She's taking my job. She's inheriting my position. You need to stop that from happening and you need to stop it now.

Nora   I don't have the slightest idea –

Krogstad   You need to persuade your husband to allow me to keep my position and to prevent Kristine Linde from working in that bank.

Nora   How could I possibly persuade my –

Krogstad   You have your ways. Think of something.

I've known old Torvald from since he was a student. He'd do anything for the attention of a lady.

Nora   If you say one more word about my husband I will show you the door.

Krogstad   Look at you. You think you're brave.

Nora   I'm not afraid of you.

Krogstad   Mrs Helmer. I will do everything I can to keep my job. I will stop at nothing.

She looks at him.

I made a mistake once too, you know. When I was younger. You probably heard about it? Did you?

She says nothing.

It never went to court. But it changed everything. From the day I was found out, from that day forward every door was closed to me. That's when I started in this line of trade. I had to do something, Mrs Helmer. I don't think I'm so bad, you know?

Nora   Don't you?

Krogstad   I think there are plenty worse.

I've learned from it. It's prepared me for my position in the bank rather elegantly. It's served as a kind of apprenticeship. I can't do it any more. My sons are growing up. I need to get my respectability back. For their sakes, not for mine. My job at the bank was the first step in that direction. If your husband gets his way I'll end up back in the gutter.

Nora   Mr Krogstad, there's nothing I can do.

Krogstad   I don't believe you. You just don't want to. It doesn't matter. I can force you.

She looks at him for a time.

Nora   You wouldn't tell him that I owed you money.

Krogstad   Wouldn't I?

Nora   You wouldn't dare. It would be so humiliating.

Krogstad   Humiliation? Is that what worries you?

She turns from him.

Nora   Well, tell him then! Show yourself for the man you are. See what my husband makes of you then.

Krogstad   Are you really just worried about the humiliation?

Nora   He'll pay you what you're owed and that will be the end of you in that bank and in this town.

Krogstad   Mrs Helmer. Have you any idea what you've done?

Nora   What in heaven's name are you talking about now?

A pause.
Krogstad *examines her.*

He smiles.

Krogstad   When your husband was, shall we say 'ill'? When your husband was a little bit ill you borrowed nearly ten thousand from me.

Nora   I didn't know anybody else.

Krogstad   I got you the money on certain conditions. Maybe your husband was so 'tired' and 'poorly' that you didn't really pay a great deal of attention to what those conditions were. You wrote me an IOU, do you remember?

Nora   Of course I remember.

Krogstad   Good. And in this IOU, this contract of debt, there were lines of guarantee that were signed by your father, do you remember those as well?

Jolly good.

And the date was left blank near the signature of guarantee for your father to complete – do you remember that too?

I gave you the IOU. You were to post it to your father. You did that straight away. Six days later you came back with the contract signed and the guarantee signed and dated and the amount was paid to you.

Nora   And I've kept up with every last payment, Mr Krogstad.

Krogstad   It must have been a very hard time for you, Mrs Helmer. Your father was very ill, was he not?

She says nothing.

Answer me. Your father was very ill, was he not?

Nora   He died shortly afterwards.

Krogstad   Yes. Tell me. Mrs Helmer. Do you remember the date of your father's death?

Nora   The twenty-ninth of September.

He takes out the contract and examines it while he talks.

Krogstad   See. I knew that. I checked it. And that's why
I have this little problem. I can't for the life of me explain it.
Because if you look – Can you see? Your father signed this
guarantee on the contract three days after he died. He died,
as you said, on the twenty-ninth of September. He signed the
contract on the second of October.

How the devil did he manage that?

And if you look, here, have a look. The handwriting for the
words 'second of October' – do you recognise that
handwriting, Mrs Helmer? Because I do.

So.

He signed it. He forgot to date it. He died. You dated it. Not
a big problem. It can happen. Perfectly common as a matter
of fact.

As long as he signed it himself.

That's all that really matters and, well, that is his signature,
isn't it, Mrs Helmer?

Isn't it, Mrs Helmer?

Mrs Helmer, that is your father's signature, isn't it?

Nora   No. It's not. I signed it in his name.

Krogstad *stares at her.*

Nora   What are you going to do about it? You'll get your
money. I'll get the contract back. I don't see that you can
possibly do anything else about it. I don't see what possible
hold you imagine you have over me.

Krogstad   Mrs Helmer, do you realise what you've just said?

Nora   What are you talking about?

Krogstad   Can I ask you, why didn't you send the contract
to your father?

Nora   It was impossible. He was too ill. He would have
wanted to know why I needed the money. I couldn't have told
him that my husband's life was in danger.

Krogstad You would have been better off giving up on your little trip to Italy.

Did it not cross your mind that you were committing an act of fraud against me?

Nora No, Mr Krogstad. It didn't cross my mind at all. After the way you treated me when I first asked you for a loan, I frankly didn't really think about you for a second more than was absolutely necessary.

Krogstad What you did is no less a crime than the crime that ruined me completely. Are you aware of that?

Nora I was saving my husband's life.

Krogstad The law is not interested in motives, Mrs Helmer.

Nora Then the law is an abomination.

Krogstad Abomination or not, it is the law that will judge you when I present this contract to the court.

Nora Is it against the law for a daughter to spare her dying father from anxiety and fear? Is it against the law for a wife to save her husband's life? I doubt that very much, Mr Krogstad. If you don't understand the difference between what I did for my husband and what you did to your wife then, well, you must be a very bad lawyer indeed.

He smiles at her.

Krogstad That may be so. But I am a very good businessman, Mrs Helmer. And let me assure you: you can do whatever you like but if I am thrown into the gutter for a second time then I will bring you down there with me.

Have a very good day and may I take this opportunity to wish a very happy Christmas to you and your family.

He leaves.

She stands for a while watching the space he has left.
She shakes her head.
She laughs.

She stops laughing.
She starts folding her children's clothes.
Jon *comes running in.*

Jon   Mummy, Anna found Ivar really quickly but she looked and looked and she couldn't find me and in the end I got bored so I had to come out and tell her where I was hiding.

Ivar *comes in.*

Ivar   She was pretending. Don't you know when somebody's pretending?

Jon   She wasn't.

Ivar   Mummy, will you play?

Nora   Not now, darling.

Ivar   Mummy, you promised.

Nora   I know. I'm sorry. I've just so much to do.

Jon   Anna's better anyway. She can find Ivar easily. She can't find me at all.

He runs off calling.

Anna. I'm coming. Ready or not!

Ivar   You're always promising and then having so much to do.

Nora   Ivar.

He leaves.
She moves to follow him.
She stops.
She sits down.
She stands up.
She thinks.
She calls.

Nora   Helene.

Helene *enters.*

Helene   Yes, ma'am.

Nora   Could you bring the tree in here?

Helene   In here?

Nora   Yes please, Helene. In here.

Helene   Very good.

She watches **Helene** *leave.*
She waits.
She shakes her head.

Nora (*whispering*)   No. No. No. No. No.

Helene *comes back struggling a little with the Christmas tree.*

Helene   Where should I set it down?

Nora   There. Right in the middle of the floor.

Helene *sets it down in the middle of the floor.*

Nora   To the right a little bit. Your left. My right. Thank you Helene. That's perfect.

Helene   Will I fetch you anything else?

Nora   No thank you, Helene. I have everything I need. That'll be all. Thank you so much.

Helene *leaves.*
Nora *sets about taking candles and flowers from a box and decorating the tree.*

Nora   Nonsense. Nonsense. Nonsense.

I will sing for you. I will dance for you.

Torvald *enters with a bundle of papers under his arm.*

Nora   You're back?

Torvald   I am. Did anybody call for me?

Nora   No. Not that I'm aware of.

Torvald   How strange. I saw Krogstad coming out into the street.

Nora   Oh, Krogstad. Yes. That's true. He was here for a moment.

He looks at her.

Torvald   Look at you.

Nora   What about me?

Torvald   It's written all over your face.

Nora   What is?

He approaches her.

Torvald   He came here to ask you to put a good word in for him, didn't he?

Nora *nods.*

Torvald   And you had to pretend that it was all your idea. Didn't you? He even asked you to pretend he hadn't spoken to you at all, didn't he?

Nora   Yes. He did, but –

Torvald   How could you agree to something like that? With a man like him?

Nora   Torvald.

Torvald   And then lie to me.

Nora   Lie?

Torvald   You told me nobody had been here.

Nora   I'm sorry.

Torvald   Your little face.

He goes to her. He touches her cheek.

My little bluebird is never to do that to me again. Is that clear? My little bluebird is going to try her very hardest to keep her little nose clean and fly ever so high in the sky and sing only sweet little pure notes from now on. Isn't she?

He holds her. She rests her head on his chest.

It's so nice in here. It's so cosy.

She smiles. She kisses him. Then backs away a touch.

Nora Torvald.

Torvald Yes.

Nora I can't wait for the party. Fancy dress!

Torvald I can't wait to see what you're going to surprise me with.

He puts the papers down on the table and sits to read them.

Nora I can't think of anything.

Torvald No?

Nora I can't think of anything that's going to work anyway. Everything I think of is silly and boring.

Torvald Is that right?

Nora Are you really, terribly, terribly busy Torvald?

Torvald Are you trying to distract me?

Nora No. What work have you got to do?

Torvald Bank work.

Nora Already?

Torvald I need to prepare the staffing changes for the New Year. I want it to be finished before I take up my office.

Nora Was that why Mr Krogstad needed to talk to you?

He doesn't answer.
She leans over him. She rubs his shoulders. She runs her hand upwards through the back of his hair.

If you weren't so busy I might have asked you to do something for me, Torvald.

Torvald Might you indeed?

She kisses the back of his neck.

Nora You know how I want to look good for you at the party?

Torvald Yes.

Nora I wondered if you wanted to help me choose my costume.

Torvald Well. I might be able to come up with one or two ideas.

Nora I'm sure you could. You're so kind. And clever. And wise.

She goes back to tending the Christmas tree, leaving him struggling to concentrate on his work.

I think the red flowers look beautiful against the green, Torvald, don't you?

He carries on working.

Torvald, will you tell me what Krogstad did that is so awful?

He continues to work as he talks.

Torvald He forged signatures.

Nora Did he?

Torvald Do you understand how bad that is?

Nora Maybe he had no choice.

Torvald I'm sorry?

Nora Maybe he found himself in a situation and the only thing he could do to get out of it was to forge the signatures.

Torvald Or maybe he was just reckless. And thoughtless. And stupid.

He carries on working.
He looks up.

I wouldn't be so angry if he'd confessed.

Nora Confessed?

Torvald And taken his, his, his punishment. But he didn't confess. He tried to trick his way out of it. He tried to use cunning. It's the trickery and the cunning that corrupts him.

Nora   Corrupts?

Torvald   Can you imagine how much he lied? Can you imagine how much he pretended to everyone? The mask he would have worn over everything. Even those closest to him. Even to his wife, Nora. Even to his children. Lying to his children is the worst thing he did.

Nora   Why?

Torvald   To lie in a family home diseases the place. It contaminates it. The children can, they can breathe it. I saw it as a lawyer. The amount of criminals I worked with who came from criminal families. The liars I worked with came from parents who lied. The thieves had thieves for fathers. And for mothers. Actually mothers are the worst. But fathers are just as bad. Krogstad knew that. He saw it too. And yet he went home and lied in front of his own children knowing all the time that he was contaminating them and what effect it would have for the rest of their lives.

I'm sorry. It exercises me.

Nora   I can tell that.

Torvald   Please. Don't try to speak up for him any more. Please don't.

He carries on working. He looks back up.

I tell you, Nora, it would have been impossible for me to work with him. I would have felt physically sick.

Nora   It's getting quite warm in here now. Is it me or is it a bit too warm?

He starts packing up his papers. He smiles at her. He goes to her.

Torvald. I've got so much to do. I've not nearly finished the tree yet. My goodness.

Torvald   I'm sorry. I can't help myself.

He backs away from her.

I'll work in my room. I need to read these before dinner

anyway and the thought of imagining your new costume, well,
I'm finding it frankly rather distracting. And I might also have
to find a time to sneak out when no soft little eyes are peeking
and put something wrapped in a little golden envelope high up
in the tree where only my skylark can find it.

She turns to him. Smiles.

The things you do to me.

He leaves.
She freezes quite still.

Nora   It's not true. It's not true. It's not true. It's not true.

Anna *enters.*

Anna   I'm so sorry to bother you. Jon and Ivar have been
asking very sweetly if you can come and play with them.

Nora   No. No. No. No. Don't let them see me. They mustn't
see me, Anna. They simply can't. You have to stay with them.

Anna   Is something wrong?

Nora   Nothing. Nothing whatsoever is wrong, Anna.
I simply want you to play with the children, which I think is
what you're paid to do, is it not?

Anna   Very good.

She leaves.
Nora *is left alone for some time.*

Two

The living room. Christmas Day.
The tree has been stripped and plundered.
It stands in the corner by the piano.
The candles have burned down.

Nora's *coat lies on the sofa.*

Nora *is alone. She paces the room. She approaches the sofa. She picks up her coat.*

She stops.

She thinks she hears something.

She moves towards the door. She listens.

She steps away from the door.

She thinks. She goes back to the door, opens it and looks out. She closes the door.

She thinks.

She calms down.

She tries to smile.

Anna *enters.*

Anna   I found the box with the costumes in.

Nora   Thank you, Anna.

Anna   Finally.

Nora   Could you put it on the table for me?

Anna   They're in an awful mess.

Nora   If I had my way, Anna, I'd tear every last one of them up into a hundred thousand pieces.

Anna *looks at her.*

Anna   I think they can be mended.

Nora   I'm sure.

Anna   A bit of patience.

Nora   I'll ask Mrs Linde to help me.

Anna   Are you going out again? It's so horrible out there. You'll get ill.

Nora   Maybe that wouldn't be such a bad thing.

How are the children?

Anna   They're playing with their presents.

Nora   They're not still asking after me, are they?

Anna   They're used to having you around.

Nora   Yes. Well. I'm afraid they're going to have to get used to not having me around quite so often any more.

Anna *looks at her.*

Anna   They're little. Little children get used to all sorts of things very quickly.

Nora   Do you think so?

Anna   I rather know so.

Nora   Do you think they'd forget me if I disappeared for ever?

Anna   I'm sorry, Mrs Helmer?

Nora   Can you tell me something, Anna? There's something I've often wondered about. How did you cope when you gave your baby away?

Anna   I didn't have much choice. I was going to go and work as a nanny for my little Nora.

Nora   But you wanted to do that, didn't you?

Anna   After what her father did to me? And then him leaving me with nothing?

Nora *thinks.*

Nora   Has she forgotten you, do you think?

Anna   No. I don't think she has. She wrote to me to tell me she was about to be confirmed. She wrote to me again after she was married.

Nora   Anna, you were such a good mother to me.

Anna   You were so little. You didn't have anybody else, my dear.

Nora   And if Ivar and Jon and Emmy, if they had nobody else I know that you would – Listen to me. I'm being stupid. Stupid. Stupid. Stupid.

She goes to the costume box.

Will you go to them, Anna. I have to start –

Tomorrow you will see how beautiful I can be.

Anna   You will be the most beautiful woman there, Nora.

She leaves.

Nora *unpacks the box.*
She takes out several costumes.
She looks at them.
She tries tearing one, it won't tear.
She throws them back in the box.

If only – If only – If only – Stupid. No one. Don't think about it. Forget it.

She closes her eyes.

One, two, three, four, five, six.

She hears something.
She starts.
She goes towards the door.
She stands there.
She listens.

Kristine *enters.*

Nora   Kristine. It's you.

Kristine   You came round while I was out.

Nora   Is there anybody else out there?

Kristine   Anybody else? No. Not that I know of.

Nora   You need to help me.

Kristine   To help you?

Nora   Let's sit down. Look. Kristine.

Kristine *looks at her, waits.*

Nora   There is a fancy dress party on tomorrow evening upstairs at the Stenborgs'. Torvald told me that he wanted very much for me to dress as a gypsy. A 'Romany dancing girl' were his exact words. He wants me to dance the tarantella. Did you know that I could dance the tarantella? I don't imagine that you did, did you? I learnt it in Capri.

Kristine   I see.

Nora   Torvald wants me to give a, a, a performance. I found the costume. He had it made for me when we were there. But look at it. It's torn to pieces. I just don't know how –

Kristine   The trimmings have come undone. I can fix that. That's easy. Have you got a needle and some black thread?

Nora *fetches her a needle and thread.*

Kristine   That's perfect.

Nora   Thank you, Kristine. That's so kind of you.

Kristine *starts sewing.* **Nora** *watches her.*

Kristine   You're going to be so dressed up, Nora.

She carries on sewing. **Nora** *watches her. Smiles.*

Kristine   I'll have to come over and have a look at you in your costume.

She carries on sewing. **Nora** *watches her.*

Kristine   I had such a lovely evening last night. Thank you.

Nora   Did you think so?

Kristine   I'm so grateful.

Nora   It's funny, because it's usually much more lovely than that, I think. You should have got here sooner, Kristine.

Kristine *carries on sewing.* **Nora** *watches her.*

Nora   Torvald certainly knows how to make his home very fine and pleasant.

Kristine   And you do too, I think. It's your father in you.

She carries on sewing. **Nora** *watches her.*

Kristine   Nora, tell me. Is Dr Rank always as depressed as he was yesterday?

Nora   No. Yesterday he was quite bad. But. The shame is that he has rather a horrible illness. His spine is wasting away. His father was – His father kept mistresses. Dr Rank inherited his father's illness at birth, I'm afraid.

Kristine *puts the sewing down.*

Kristine   Nora. How do you know about something like that?

Nora   I've had three children, Kristine. When you've had children, like I have then, well – you are sometimes visited by, let us say by ladies who have a certain knowledge of medicine. They tell all kinds of stories.

Kristine *carries on sewing. Silence for a time.*

Kristine   Does Dr Rank visit every day?

Nora   Every day. He's Torvald's oldest friend. He's my friend too. It's like he belongs here.

Kristine   Can I ask you, Nora, is he an honest man? Is he not something of a flatterer?

Nora   No. Quite the opposite. Why on earth do you ask that?

Kristine   Yesterday. When you introduced me to him he told me that he had often heard my name mentioned. But Torvald didn't seem to have the slightest idea who I was.

Nora   That's Torvald. He's so unthinkably fond of me that he wants to keep me all to himself. He used to be quite jealous if I even mentioned the names of anybody from back home. So I stopped mentioning them. But I've always spoken to Dr Rank about things like that because he rather likes to hear about them.

Kristine *pauses in her sewing and looks at* **Nora**.

Kristine   Nora. I'm going to say something to you. I'm a little bit older than you.

Nora   Not really much older.

Kristine   I've a touch more experience. I think you should get out of your relationship with Dr Rank.

Nora   What do you mean, 'my relationship'?

Kristine   I mean everything. Yesterday you talked about your rich admirer who would give you money to –

Nora   A made-up rich admirer, who exists only in my head.

Kristine   Is Dr Rank rich?

Nora   Yes, he is.

Kristine   And with no family. No obligations. No one to provide for?

Nora   No, no one.

Kristine   And he comes here every day?

Nora   I told you that.

Kristine   How can such a fine man be so crude?

Nora   I don't have the slightest idea what you're talking about.

Kristine   Nora, don't pretend I haven't guessed who lent you the money.

Nora   Have you gone mad?

Kristine *pauses in her sewing. She looks up at* **Nora**.

Nora   How could you think I'd ever do something like that? He's our best friend.

Kristine   It wasn't him?

Nora   No, it wasn't. I would never have dreamt – He didn't have the money in those days anyway. He inherited it a long time after –

Kristine   Well I think that's a relief, for you Nora. I really do.

Nora   A relief? I would never have asked Jens.

Kristine *carries on sewing.* **Nora** *watches her.*

Nora   Although I have to say I'm fairly sure that if I did ask him –

Kristine   You mustn't.

Nora   I won't. But I know that if I did speak to him –

Kristine   Behind Torvald's back?

Nora   I'm playing out this whole horrible mess behind Torvald's back. I don't see how that's different to talking to Dr Rank.

Kristine   Nora. I just want you to be careful.

Nora   A man can manage these things much better than a woman – is that what you're saying?

That's not true.

That's complete rubbish.

Kristine *stares at her.*

Nora   When you pay off a debt your contract of debt is returned to you, in law, is it not?

Kristine   Yes, it is.

Nora   And then if you want you can tear it into a hundred thousand pieces and burn it, can't you? If that's what you want to do?

Kristine   You're hiding something from me.

Nora   Hiding something from you? What do you mean? How can you tell?

Kristine   Something's happened. What is it?

Nora   Kristine.

She hears something.

Shhh. It's Torvald. He's home.

Kristine   Nora?

Nora   Please. Can you, can you, can you go and see the children for a while?

Torvald hates seeing sewing left lying around the house. He hates it. Let Anna help you.

Kristine   Anna?

Nora   Please, Kristine. Please don't ask anything more. Please go and see the children. Please take the sewing to Anna. If he sees the sewing left just lying there he'll – Sewing!

Kristine   Nora. Please. I will go and see the children. Of course I will. I will take the sewing away with me. I'll clear it away completely. But I'm not leaving until we've finished this conversation.

Kristine *exits.*
Nora *prepares herself.*
Torvald *enters from the hall.*

Torvald   Was that the dressmaker?

Nora   No. It was Kristine. She's helping me mend my costume. You're lucky I like indulging you so much.

He takes her chin in his hand.

Torvald Lucky? I'm your husband. It's your job to indulge
me. You funny little creature.

He kisses her.

I won't disturb you. You probably need to try that costume
of yours on or something, have a little practice or what-not,
don't you?

Nora And you probably need to go and do more work.

He shows her his papers.

Torvald I've been in the bank all morning.

He heads to his study.

Nora Torvald.

Torvald Nora.

Nora If your little swallow were to swoop down from up in
the sky and ask you to do something for her in her prettiest
voice would you do it?

Torvald It depends on what it was.

Nora Your swallow would get ever so excited if you did.

Torvald It still depends on what it was.

Nora She would sing and sing and sing for you.

Torvald You sing for me all day anyway.

Nora She'd turn into a little fairy. She'd dance for you in the
moonlight.

Torvald Nora – this isn't about what we talked about this
morning, is it?

Nora Torvald, please.

Torvald I can't believe you've got the nerve to even think
about asking me again.

Nora Torvald, you must listen to me. Krogstad –

Torvald   Nora. Don't. I told you.

And anyway.

It's his job I've given to Mrs Linde.

Nora   Then get rid of somebody else.

Torvald   Nora, just because you made some stupid little promise to a man like him doesn't mean for one second that I would even think about –

Nora   I'm not thinking about the promise. I'm thinking about you. I'm thinking about what he could do to you. He could tell people all manner of things about you. He could write to the papers about you. He could really harm you. I'm terrified of him.

He looks at her.

Torvald   Ah. I see. I see what's happening here.

Nora   What?

Torvald   He reminds you of what happened to your father.

Nora   People were so vicious. They slandered him, Torvald. He would have been sacked if it hadn't been you who'd been sent to investigate him. You were so kind.

Torvald   Nora. There is such a difference between your father and I.

Nora   I know that.

Torvald   I think in comparison to your father, my reputation as a public figure is unimpeachable. I'm fairly determined to keep it that way.

Nora   You have no idea how evil people can be.

Torvald, I'm begging you.

Torvald   It's too late. Everybody knows I'm dismissing him. If word got round that I changed my mind just because my wife begged me –

Nora   What would happen?

Torvald   I'd be a laughing stock. People would think I was weak. That can never happen. And anyway –

Nora   What?

Torvald   I might be able to overlook his immorality in a time of emergency.

Nora   I think you really could.

Torvald   And I gather he can be skilled at his work. But he is a friend from my youth. I should never have made his acquaintance, of course, but I was young. Honestly Nora, we were on first-name terms. And he's so tactless. He doesn't even pretend to hide it. He strolls around talking about me as though I'm his closest friend. 'Torvald does this. Torvald thinks that.' It's embarrassing. He would make my life and my work completely intolerable.

Nora   You don't mean that.

Torvald   What do you mean, 'I don't mean it'?

Nora   Those reasons are petty.

Torvald   Nora, did you just say that I was 'petty'?

Nora   No. I said the reasons are petty. That's different. It's precisely because you're not petty that the reasons make no sense coming out of your mouth.

Torvald   I never thought I'd hear you say something like that about me.

This ends. Right now.

He goes to the door and shouts.

Helene.

Nora   Torvald.

Then he takes out some papers and writes a note, puts it in an envelope and addresses it.

Torvald   Helene.

Nora   What are you doing?

Torvald   I'm making a decision.

Nora   Torvald, please.

Torvald   Helene, for heaven's sake.

Helene *enters.*

Torvald   Helene. Take this letter. Go downstairs right now. Have it delivered immediately.

Helene   Yes, sir.

Torvald   Straight away, Helene. I mean it.

Helene   Yes, sir. I'm going, sir.

She leaves. **Nora** *stares at him.*

Torvald   There. All done.

Nora *stares at him.*

Nora   What was in that letter?

Torvald   Krogstad's dismissal.

Nora   No. No. No. Call it back. It's not too late. Torvald, please. For me. For, for, for your own sake. For the children. You have no idea what this could do to us.

Torvald   It's too late, Nora.

Nora   It can't be.

Torvald   It is.

I forgive you, you know?

Nora   Forgive me?

Torvald   Your fear. Is actually rather insulting. Isn't it? To think that I should worry about the wittering of a depraved clerk. But I do. I forgive you. You must love me so much.

He takes her in his arms.

Which is exactly how it should be.

He kisses her.

Let's see what happens shall we?

Let me tell you, though, when the real crises come I will prove to you that I have both the strength and courage to face them. You'll see what kind of man I can be then.

Nora   What do you mean?

Torvald   I mean exactly what I say.

Nora   You don't have to prove anything to me.

Torvald   No?

Nora   Of course you don't.

Torvald   We'll face it together then, should we? As man and wife.

He caresses her face.

Shhh. Calm down. Your little eyes! You look like a frightened little dove. All these thoughts inside your head.

He rests his finger on her lips.

Now. Isn't it time for you to do some practising? Don't you think it's time to go and practise the tarantella? You need to be ready by tomorrow night. I'll close my door. I won't hear a thing. You can make as much noise as you want.

He leaves her.
He stops at his doorway.

When Rank gets here, he knows where he can find me.

He goes into his office.
She is left alone. She stands completely still. As though nailed to the floor.

Nora   Oh. Oh. Oh. Oh. He will do it.

Never.

Before everything. Whatever happens.

The bell rings.

She hears it.
She wipes her face. She goes to the door.
Rank *is hanging up his coat in the hallway.*

As they talk it begins to get dark.

Nora   I knew it was you. I recognised the way you rang the bell.

Rank *enters.*

Nora   Torvald asked me to ask you if you could wait for a short while. He is finishing some business for the bank.

Rank   Terribly important business, I have no doubt. And what about you, Nora? Are you dreadfully busy as well?

She closes the door behind him.

Nora   I always have time for you, Dr Rank. You know that.

Rank   I'm glad. I'll make sure I take advantage of that for as long as I can.

Nora   What do you mean, for as long as you can?

Rank   My dear Nora, you sound rather frightened by the idea.

Nora   Well it was rather a strange expression, Doctor. 'For as long as I can.'

Rank   It may not be as long as I'd hoped for, Nora. It seems that something I've been preparing myself for, for rather a long time, may actually be starting to happen.

She goes to him. She clasps his arm.

Nora   What's happened?

Rank   Everything's downhill from here on in, I'm afraid. There is, it seems, nothing to be done.

Nora   You must tell me –

Rank   I am the most miserable of all my patients, Mrs Helmer. Over the past few days I've been totting up my internal accounts. I find them to be bankrupt. Within the next month, Nora my dear, I could well be rotting away in some churchyard or other.

Nora   Don't talk like that. That's horrible.

Rank   Well, it's something of a horrible situation I'm afraid. And the worst thing is that it will only get far more horrible. There is just one examination left for me to undergo. When that's done I'll have a pretty good idea when the end will start. When the disintegration will begin.

There is something I want to tell you. Helmer has such a delicate sensibility. He has such a fine nature. He has an aversion against everything ugly. I don't want him to be there –

She stops him. She squeezes his arm.

I will lock my door to him. As soon as I know for certain I will send a visiting card to you. I will draw a black cross on it. Then you will know.

Nora   You're just being – This is unreasonable.

Rank   Am I demonstrating a lack of reason as I face my own death? Oh, how miserably inconsiderate of me!

Nora   I really rather need you to be in a good mood today.

Rank   What is happening to me is not in any way fair.

He looks at her. He looks away. He smiles.

Maybe it's the same for everybody, Nora. Maybe all parents leave a curse for their children to inherit. Maybe it's unavoidable. Certainly it's merciless.

Nora   That's nonsense. You just need to cheer yourself up.

He looks at her for some time.

Rank   Do you think so?

Maybe you're right. Maybe the only choice one has in such circumstances is to laugh. My poor, innocent spine it seems must pay the price for my father's rather jolly days in the army.

Ha!

Nora   He was rather partial to asparagus and *pâté de foie gras*, was he not?

Rank   Absolutely, he was. And truffles.

Nora   Yes. Truffles. And oysters too, I believe?

Rank   Oh God yes, oysters. He was deeply partial to the occasional oyster was my father.

Nora   And then there's all the port and the champagne. Why is it, Dr Rank, that the most delicious things affect the spine so very badly?

Rank   Especially a poor unhappy spine like mine that never had the opportunity to sample all those delicious things for itself.

Nora   Yes. That is the saddest thing of all.

He smiles at her.

Rank   Hm.

Nora   What are you smiling at?

Rank   I'm not smiling. You're smiling.

Nora   No, you are.

Rank   You're a mischief-maker, Mrs Helmer. You're a bigger mischief-maker than even I realised.

Nora   I'm in a bit of a mad mood today.

Rank   I can tell that.

She goes to him. She rests her hands on his shoulders.

Nora   My beautiful, dear, own Dr Rank. You're not going to go and die on me and Torvald.

Rank   You'll recover from it, Nora. Fairly quickly I would have thought. Once gone, soon forgotten. As it were.

She looks at him, says nothing.

People do recover from these things, you know?
They make new friends. They build new relationships.

Nora   Who builds new relationships?

Rank   You will. You and Torvald will. After I've gone. You've started already of course, so it would seem. What on earth was this so-called Mrs Linde doing here last night?

Nora   Are you jealous of poor Kristine?

Rank   Yes, I am. She will succeed me in this house. When I've died I have no doubt that that woman –

Nora   Ssshh. Keep your voice down. She's in there.

Rank   Is she indeed? Back again. You see what I mean?

Nora   She's mending my costume for tomorrow night. You're impossible, you really are.

Please be nice to me.

You just wait until tomorrow. You'll see how beautifully I can dance. I'll dance and you can imagine that I'm dancing just for you.

And Torvald. Of course. That goes without saying.

She takes some things out of the costume box.

Sit down. I want to show you something.

He sits down.

Rank   What is it?

Nora   Here.

Rank   Silk stockings.

Nora   Aren't they lovely? It's getting dark. You can't see properly in here. Wait until tomorrow night. You'll see them then. No. No. No you won't. You're only allowed to see my feet. Well. I'll let you look a little bit higher.

What? Why are you looking like that?

Don't you think they'll fit me?

Rank   There is no way I could possibly tell that from here.

Nora *does a little fake gasp.*

Nora   Dr Rank!

She hits him playfully on the ear with the stockings.

You should be ashamed of yourself.

Rank   And what other little treats will I get tomorrow night?

Nora   None. No more treats. You're being too naughty.

She hums a little tune.
She searches among the costumes in the box.
He watches her for some time.

Rank   Sometimes, Nora. When I look at you. When I sit with you. As closely as this. I just can't understand, I can't possibly imagine what my life would have been if I'd never come into this house.

She smiles at him.

And the idea of having to leave it all –

Nora   You don't have to leave it.

Rank   – without having left any mark or trace, without having left any proof of having even been here. Not even as a sign of gratitude. I'll leave nothing but an empty space. That can be filled in by anybody.

She looks at him. Some time.

Nora   What if I were to ask you – ?

Rank   What?

Nora   No, I couldn't.

Rank   What couldn't you ask? Tell me.

Nora   For a proof of your friendship. No. I don't mean that.

Rank   If I could do anything for you, you know how happy that would make me.

Nora   You have no idea what I'm going to ask you, yet.

Rank   It doesn't matter. Say it.

Nora   I can't. It would be too much. I need your advice. I need your help. I need you to do something for me.

Rank   I have absolutely no idea what you're talking about. You need to be a touch more explicit. Nora, don't you trust me?

Nora   I trust you more than anybody else I know. You are my most faithful friend. You are my truest friend. You know that.

Dr Rank; I need you to help me stop something from happening. You know how much Torvald loves me. There is not a moment when he wouldn't give up his whole life for my sake.

Rank   Nora. Do you imagine for a second that he is the only man who would do that for you?

Nora   What do you mean?

Rank   Nora I swore to myself that I would tell you before I left you. I'm telling you now.

Do you imagine that Torvald Helmer is the only man who would die for you because I can assure you, most vehemently, that he is not.

So.

Now you know.

And now you know you can confide in me more than anybody else in the world.

She stands up.

Nora   Can you let me pass please.

Rank   Nora.

Nora   I need to get past.

He lets her past.

Helene. Helene, could you bring the lamp please.

That was awful. You shouldn't have said that.

Rank   I have loved you as much as anybody else in the world. I don't see why that is anything to be ashamed of.

Nora   You shouldn't have told me. You didn't even need to tell me.

Rank   Did you know?

Helene *enters. She has a lamp. She notices the atmosphere in the room. She tries her hardest to be invisible which makes her more visible than ever. She puts the lamp down. She leaves.*

Rank   I asked you, did you know how I felt about you?

Nora   I've no idea any more. I've no idea how – how do people know what they know and what they don't know? I can't believe you could be so stupid, Dr Rank.

Rank   No.

Nora   When everything was going so well.

Rank   At least you know you can trust me completely. At least there's that. Now maybe you can tell me what you were going to say.

Nora   Not any more.

Rank   Nora, I'm begging you.

Nora   I'm not telling you anything now.

Rank   Please don't punish me. I would do anything for you that is humanly possible.

Nora   It's too late. You can't do anything for me now. I don't need help really anyway. It was just something I made up. It wasn't even real. It was all in my head.

She looks at him in the light. She smiles.

Look at you. All lit up like that. Do you feel a bit silly now?

Rank   No.

Nora   Do you feel terribly ashamed of yourself?

Rank   No, I don't. I think I'm going to go.

Nora   Come back soon.

Rank   I rather think I might not.

Nora   Yes, you will. You always do. You must, anyway.
You know Torvald can't live without you.

Rank   What about you?

Nora   Oh, I always have such tremendous fun when you
come round.

Rank   I think I've been rather misled. I'm afraid I was under
the illusion that you enjoyed being with me as much as you
enjoyed being with your husband.

Nora   But that's true. I do. That's not an illusion at all. Don't
you find that's true of life, though, Dr Rank? In life we have
the people we are fond of and the people we enjoy being with.

It's like when I lived at home I was so deeply fond of my
father. But I always thought it was much more fun sneaking
down to the maids. They never told me what to do. They
always had such fun together.

Rank   I've taken the place of the maids. I see that now.

Nora   That's not what I meant.

Please. Dr Rank. Don't be cross with me.

You can see what I mean about Torvald being like my father,
though, can't you.

Rank *smiles at her.*
Helene *enters.*

Helene   Madam.

Rank *and* **Nora** *look at her.*

Helene *whispers to her. She hands her a business card.* **Nora** *puts it
in her pocket.*

Nora   Thank you.

Helene   Not at all.

She leaves.

Rank   Is there something wrong?

Nora   No. No. No. It's just something – It's my new costume.

Rank   I thought Mrs Linde in there was mending your costume.

Nora   Yes, she is. My old one. I bought a new one. Shhh. Don't tell Torvald.

Rank   So. Another big secret from your husband. How exciting.

Nora   Isn't it? Dr Rank. You must distract him for me. Will you? Go to him. He should be ready for you now. He's in his study. Keep him in there for a while. Don't let him suspect anything.

Rank   Don't worry. He'll get nothing out of me. I promise you.

Nora –

Nora   Quick. Hurry. Before he comes out.

He smiles at her.

Rank   Yes. Of course.

He leaves.
A beat.

Nora   Helene.

She enters.

Is he still in the kitchen?

Helene   He came up through the –

Nora   Did you tell him I had a visitor?

Helene   I tried. It made no difference.

Nora   Won't he leave?

Helene   Not until he's spoken to you, he said.

Nora   Then bring him in. Tell him he must be quiet. And Helene, you can't tell anybody. Not even Anna. I, I, I'm planning a surprise for my husband.

Helene   Very good. I understand completely.

She smiles. She gets excited by the idea of keeping a secret. She leaves.
Nora *is alone.*
She locks the door to her husband's study as quietly as she can.
She waits.
Krogstad *enters. He is dressed for a cold day outside.*

Nora   You have to be quiet. My husband's in his office.

Krogstad   That doesn't matter to me at all.

Nora   What do you want?

Krogstad   I need to find out something.

Nora   What?

Krogstad *smiles.*

Nora   Hurry up. What do you want to find out?

Krogstad   I suppose you know that I've been dismissed from the bank.

Nora   I couldn't prevent it. I did everything I could.

Krogstad   He must think very little of you, your husband. He knows what I can do to you and he doesn't seem to –

Nora   What makes you think he knows anything?

Krogstad   No. Of course he doesn't. I should have realised. If he knew he'd never dare stand up to me like this. Not Old Torvald Helmer.

Nora   Mr Krogstad, don't you dare speak like that about my husband.

Krogstad   I do beg your pardon. Am I right in presuming, therefore, since you've kept everything so hidden from him, that you've started to realise exactly how much trouble you might actually be in?

Nora   What is it you want from me?

Krogstad   I just wanted to see how you were, Mrs Helmer.
I've been worrying about you all day. Even a grubby little
moneylender like me, an inept, idiotic lawyer, even I have a
heart, Mrs Helmer.

Nora   Then maybe you could show it.

Think of my children.

Krogstad   Have you for one second ever thought about
mine? Has your husband?

No. Don't answer that. It doesn't matter. I just wanted to tell
you that you don't need to worry too much for now. I thought
I'd pop by and reassure you that I'm not going to do anything
at all about this for the time being.

Nora   Is that right?

Krogstad   I think this whole business could be dealt with
quite quietly. Just between the three of us. Nobody else needs
to know.

Nora   My husband is never going to find out anything about
any of this.

Krogstad   No? How the devil are you going to stop that
from happening? Are you going to pay off the rest of the debt?

Nora   Not immediately.

Krogstad   It wouldn't change anything anyway, you know.
Even if you had all my money in cash right there in your hand
I wouldn't give you your IOU back.

I want to keep it. I like having it around my person. Nobody
else will ever find out anything about it. In case you were
thinking about doing something desperate.

She says nothing.

In case you were thinking of running away.

She says nothing.

Or doing something a little bit more, what? Drastic, than that?

She says nothing.

Don't.

Nora   How did you know –

Krogstad   Everybody thinks about it at first, you know.
When they realise they've been cornered. It's perfectly natural.
I thought about it for a while. I couldn't do it. I got too scared.

She says nothing.

You couldn't either, could you? It would be such a stupid
thing to do. Once the shock's passed everything will blow over.
He'll calm down once he's got his head around everything.
I've written him a letter. I've got it here. It's in my pocket.
It explains everything as simply and as – what? Sensitively? As
'sensitively' as I could manage.

Nora   Please don't give it to him. Tear it up. Tear it into a
thousand pieces. I'll find you your money.

Krogstad   I'm sorry? I thought you just said –

Nora   I'm not talking about my debt. Let me know how
much you want from my husband and I will get that for you.

Krogstad   I don't want any money from him.

Nora   Then what do you want?

Krogstad   I want to get back on my feet, Mrs Helmer. I want
to get back to the top again. Your husband has to help me. I've
not done anything wrong now for two years. In all that time
I have lived in the hardest circumstances you could imagine.
I didn't mind. It didn't bother me. I was working my way up,
step by step. And now I've been kicked back down in the most
savage way I have ever known. I want a lot more than
forgiveness this time, Mrs Helmer. I want to go back to the
bank. I want your husband to create a post for me. I want a
higher position than I've ever had before.

Nora   He'll never give you that.

Krogstad   He will. I know him. He'll be too scared to do anything else. And when he does, you just watch me. I'll be his right-hand man in less than a year. And not long after that I'll be running the Savings Bank myself.

Nora   I'll never live to let that happen.

Krogstad   Mrs Helmer, you're not suggesting –

Nora   You have no idea what I am capable of doing.

Krogstad   Oh, I think I do. A delicate, spoilt, little lady like you –

Nora   I'll show you.

Krogstad   Will you?

How would you do it, Mrs Helmer? Down under the ice? Would you drown yourself in the cold, black water? Float up in the springtime all bloated and ugly.

Nora   You don't scare me.

Krogstad   No. And I'm afraid to tell you that you don't scare me a great deal either. People don't do things like that, Mrs Helmer. What would be the point, anyway? I have him completely under my thumb.

Nora   You couldn't do anything to him after I'd –

Krogstad   Couldn't I? Have you forgotten? I control the very way he would remember you.

So. There.

Don't do anything stupid, will you? I'll get this letter to Mr Helmer. I look forward to getting his reply.

Don't forget, Mrs Helmer, this is all his fault. He forced me to do what I'm doing to you. I'm afraid I'll never be able to forgive him for that.

Good day, Mrs Helmer.

He leaves.
She goes to the door.

She listens.
She hears him drop the letter in the post box.
She winces as though stung.
She contracts her body up into a knot.
Kristine *enters with the costume.*

Kristine   There. I've finished. I've mended every last stitch. It's perfect. It looks –

She sees **Nora**.

Kristine   What's happened? You look awful.

Nora   Come here.

Kristine *approaches her.*

Nora   Can you look outside into the hall for me?

Kristine   Whatever's the matter?

Nora   Can you? Please, Kristine?

Kristine *opens the door and peers down the hall.*

Nora   There. Can you see the post box? Can you look through the glass in the post box?

Kristine   Yes. Yes. I see it.

Nora   Is there a letter in there?

Kristine   Yes. I can see it from here.

Nora   The letter's from Krogstad.

Kristine *looks at her.*

Kristine   Krogstad?

Nora   Yes. Now Torvald will find out everything.

Kristine's *face falls. She realises.*

Kristine   It was Krogstad who –

Oh, believe me, Nora. In the end it will be better for both of you. I promise you.

Nora   It won't.

Kristine   It doesn't seem like that now but, Nora –

Nora   I forged a signature.

Kristine *stares at her.*

Nora   I need to tell you something. I need you to be my, my, my, my witness. I need you to be my witness.

Kristine   Witness to what?

Nora   In case I go out of my mind.

Kristine   Nora!

Nora   Or in case anything else happens to me that means I can't be around here any more.

Kristine   Nora, what are you talking about?

Nora   If anybody else tries to take the blame for what I've done then you need to be my witness that it isn't true, Kristine. I'm not mad in any way. I can see things perfectly clearly. I tell you. Nobody else knew anything about what I did. I did everything on my own.

Kristine   I don't understand.

Nora   How could you? Kristine, the most wonderful thing is about to happen.

Kristine   The most wonderful thing?

Nora   Yes. But it's so terrible, Kristine. It can't happen. Not for anything in the world.

Kristine   I'm going to talk to Krogstad now.

Nora   Don't. Don't go near him! He could really harm you.

Kristine   There was a time when he would have done anything for me.

Nora *looks at her.*

Kristine   Where does he live?

Nora *reaches into her pocket. She finds* **Krogstad**'s *card. She gives it to* **Kristine**.

Nora   Here. But the letter, the letter!

Torvald *knocks on his office door.*

Torvald (*off*)   Nora! Nora!

Nora   What is it? What do you want?

Torvald (*off*)   Don't be so scared little mouse. We can't get in.

She stares at the door.

You've locked the door Nora.

She stares at the door.

Are you trying on your costume, in there?

Nora   Yes! Yes! I am! I'm trying on my costume. It looks – I look– I'm going to look beautiful, Torvald.

Kristine   He lives just round the corner.

Nora   It doesn't matter. The letter's in the box.

Kristine   And Torvald has the key?

Nora   Of course he does.

Kristine   Krogstad must demand the letter back unread. He needs to think of an excuse as to why he –

Nora   But this is the time when Torvald checks his –

Kristine   Then stop him. I'll be back as soon as I can.

She exits.

Nora *goes to* **Torvald**'s *study. She unlocks the door.*

Nora   Torvald?

Torvald   So. Is a man finally allowed to slip back into his own drawing room? That's good. Come on, Dr Rank. Let's have a look at her.

He comes to the doorway.

What's going on?

Nora   What do you mean, Torvald?

Torvald   Dr Rank promised me a grand show.

Rank   It appears I was wrong.

Nora   Yes. You were. Nobody will get to see me in all my finery until tomorrow evening.

Torvald   Nora, darling. You look exhausted. Have you been overdoing the practising a little?

Nora   No. I've not done any yet.

Torvald   You're going to have to.

Nora   I tried, Torvald. But I can't do anything without you. I've forgotten everything.

Torvald   Oh, we'll soon sort that out.

Nora   You're going to have to take care of me, Torvald. I'm so anxious. The party's tomorrow. You must sacrifice yourself completely for me. You can't do any work tonight. I don't even want to see a pen in your hand. Do you promise me?

Torvald   Yes. I promise you; tonight I will be completely at your service.

He goes towards the doorway.

Nora   Where are you going?

Torvald   I just want to check if any letters have arrived.

Nora   No. No. Don't. Torvald.

Torvald   What's the matter?

Nora   Torvald, I beg you. There's nothing out there.

Torvald   I just need to check.

He goes to leave.
Nora *goes to the piano.*

She plays the first bars of the tarantella.
Torvald *stops.*
He turns to her. He smiles.

Nora   I won't be able to dance at all tomorrow if I don't practise with you first.

Torvald *goes to her.*

Torvald   You're so frightened!

Nora   I'm terrified. I want to practise now. Can I? There's still a bit of time before dinner. Come on. Will you sit down and play for me, Torvald? You can correct my mistakes. You can guide me.

Torvald   If you want me to, Nora, it would be a pleasure.

Nora *takes a tambourine from the box and a long, multicoloured shawl which she drapes about herself.*
She springs on to the floor.
She shouts.

Nora   Play for me! Now! I want to dance!

Torvald *plays.*
Nora *dances.*
Rank *stands by the piano behind* **Torvald** *and watches her.*

Torvald   Slow down. A little slower.

Nora   I can't go any slower.

Torvald   Don't be so violent, Nora.

Nora   I can't help myself. I have to be violent.

Torvald *stops playing.*

Torvald   No. No. That's just – It's not right at all.

Nora *laughs and swings the tambourine.*

Nora   I told you I couldn't do it.

Rank   I could play.

Torvald   Good idea. You play. Then I can guide her better.

Rank *sits at the piano and plays.*
Nora *dances. Her dancing gets more and more wild.*
Torvald *watches her dance. He tries to correct her as she dances.*

Torvald   A touch slower, Nora. Listen to the music. With the music. You're not listening.

She does not appear to hear a word he's saying.
Her hair comes loose and falls over her shoulders.
She doesn't notice.
Kristine *enters.*
She stands at the doorway.

Nora   Look, Kristine, this is such fun.

Torvald   My dear darling. You're dancing as though your life depends upon it.

Nora   It does.

Torvald   Rank. Thank you. Stop playing. This is madness. Stop. Dr Rank.

Rank *stops playing.* **Nora** *stops suddenly.*
Torvald *goes to* **Nora**.

Torvald   I can't believe it. It's like you've forgotten everything.

Nora   I told you I had.

Torvald   You need a huge amount of work and help and instruction.

Nora   I know. I really do. You have to teach me everything again, Torvald. Every last move. Will you? Do you promise me?

Torvald   Completely.

Nora   You're not allowed to think of anything else or anybody else but me. Not for the rest of the day. Not all day tomorrow. You're not allowed to do any work. Or open any letters or do anything. You're not even allowed to open the post box.

Torvald Ah.

Nora What?

Torvald You're still frightened of him.

She looks at him.

Has he written a letter to me? I can see it in your face.

Nora I don't know. He might have done. I didn't see. But you're not allowed to read it. Nothing ugly can come between us until after the party and everything is over.

Rank I wouldn't contradict her if I were you, Mr Helmer.

Torvald Very well. But tomorrow night. After you've danced.

Nora Then you're free.

Helene *enters.*

Helene Dinner is served.

Nora Helene, can you open a bottle of champagne?

Helene Certainly, ma'am.

She exits.

Torvald So. We're having a party now, are we?

Nora Yes. We are. A champagne party. We're going to drink champagne until the morning rises.

She shouts into the hall.

And get some chocolates, Helene. Huge amounts of chocolates, for everybody. Just tonight.

Torvald *goes to* **Nora**. *He clasps her hands.*

Torvald Calm down. You're getting yourself wound up. I want my skylark back.

Nora Oh, she will come back. I promise you, Torvald. Now. You two gentlemen go and sit down for our champagne dinner. Kristine needs to help me with my hair.

Rank   Torvald, is she expecting?

Torvald   My dear Dr Rank, far from it. She's just being childish. And frightened.

They leave.
Nora *looks to* **Kristine**.

Kristine   He's gone away. He's gone to the countryside.

Nora   I could tell. I could see it in your face.

Kristine   He'll be back tomorrow evening. I left him a note.

Nora   You shouldn't have done that. I'm not going to try to prevent anything any more. I'm just going to wait. Something wonderful is going to happen.

Kristine   What are you talking about?

Nora   You wouldn't understand. Even if I told you. You should go in. I'll just be a moment.

Kristine *exits.*
Nora *gathers herself.*
She looks at her watch.
She calculates how long it will be until the tarantella is over.
She thinks.
She smiles.
She closes her eyes.
She counts to ten.
Torvald *comes in.*

Torvald   What are you doing? Where's my little hamster?

Nora   She's here. She's ready.

Three

The drawing room.
The table and chairs have been moved to the middle of the floor.
The lamp has been lit.
The door to the hall is open.
Dance music can be heard from above.

Kristine *sits at the table. She tries to read a book. She can't concentrate.*
She listens.
She hears something.
She stands up.
She listens again.
She goes to the door.

Kristine   Come in here. There's no one around.

Krogstad   I got your note. I'm not entirely sure I understood it, I have to confess.

They try to control the volume of their speech throughout.

Kristine   I need to speak to you.

Krogstad   You said. Why here?

Kristine   I can't meet you at my place. You can come in. We're completely alone. The maid is asleep. The Helmers are at a party upstairs.

Krogstad   A party? Tonight? How lovely for them.

Kristine   We need to talk.

Krogstad   Do we? I can't imagine what more we could possibly have to say to one another.

Kristine   Nils, don't.

Krogstad   A woman with no heart left a man who loved her when a more financially secure position was offered to her. What more needs to be said about that?

Kristine *looks at him for a time.*

Kristine   Do you really think I have no heart?

Krogstad   None that I've seen.

Kristine   Do you really think it was that easy for me?

Krogstad   Wasn't it?

Kristine   I had no choice.

Krogstad   That wasn't what your letter said.

Kristine   I couldn't write anything else. The kindest thing I could do to you after the decisions I'd made was to kill off every feeling you ever felt for me.

Krogstad   Yes. Well. You achieved that. And then you got your money.

Kristine   I had to look after my mother and my brothers. They were desperate.

Krogstad   They may well have been. But you had no right to do that to me.

Kristine   Do you think I didn't know that? Do you think I've ever thought of anything else since?

He looks at her.

Krogstad   When you left, the earth crumbled away from beneath my feet. Look at me. I'm shipwrecked.

Kristine   I could help you.

Krogstad   There was a time I thought you could. You rather let me down.

She looks at him. Some time.

Kristine   I had no idea I was taking your job at the bank.

Krogstad   I'm sure you didn't. Are you going to resign then?

Kristine   No. It wouldn't help you anyway, even if I did.

Krogstad   I'd do it for you, if you asked me to.

Kristine   Well, that would be stupid of you. Life's hard, Nils. Life's bitter. There is no room for sentiment. I've learned that from experience.

Krogstad   Do you want to know what I've learned from experience, Kristine? Never believe a word anybody tells you.

Krogstad *looks at her.*

Kristine   You said you were shipwrecked.

Krogstad   I am.

Kristine   I am too. I have nobody left in the world.

Krogstad   You should have thought about that.

Kristine   If two shipwrecked people can reach out for each other –

Krogstad   Don't.

Kristine   It would be so much better.

Krogstad   Don't do this.

Kristine   It would be so much safer for them.

Krogstad   Kristine.

Kristine   Why do you think I even came here?

Krogstad   Please don't.

Kristine   I was looking for you. Nils, I need to work. If I'm going to survive I need to work. I've worked my whole life. It's been the one thing that has made me most happy. But I'm so alone. I'm empty, Nils. I can't work just for myself any more. I need somebody to work for.

Krogstad   You're lying.

Kristine   I'm not.

Krogstad   You're being hysterical.

Kristine   When have you ever known me to be hysterical?

Krogstad   Have you any idea how I've been living? Have you any idea of the things that I have done?

She nods.

Have you got the slightest idea what people say about me?

Kristine   That doesn't matter. People can change. People can make each other better than they are.

Krogstad   What if it's too late for that?

Kristine   It's not.

He looks at her.
She goes to him.
She touches his face.
It is like it's the first time anybody has touched his face for years and years.

I need to be somebody's mother. Your children need a mother. I know you so well. I know your core.

She kisses him.
He kisses her back.
The music upstairs stops.
She hears it.

Wait. Shhh. Listen. The music's stopped. You have to go.

Krogstad   Why? What's wrong?

Kristine   The dance has finished. The party's over. They'll be coming down.

Krogstad   You have no idea what I've done to them.

Kristine   I do.

Krogstad   Then how can you –

Kristine   I know what despair does to people. Believe me.

Krogstad   I wish I could go back in time and not have done it.

Kristine   You could.

Krogstad   What?

Kristine   Your letter is still in the box.

Krogstad   How do you know that?

She looks at him.

Are you doing this for her? Is this all for her benefit, Kristine? Tell me.

Kristine   I sold myself for the sake of other people once before. I'm never going to do it again.

Krogstad   I'll ask for my letter back.

Kristine   No. Don't.

Krogstad   I'll wait here until Torvald comes down and I will tell him he has to give me back my letter. I'll tell him that in my anger at my dismissal I wrote him a letter that I regret ever writing and that for the sake of my dignity he mustn't read it.

Kristine   You can't. You would not believe the things that I have seen happen here since last night. This secret is horrible. It's killing them. Torvald needs to be told everything.

He looks at her.

Hurry. You have to go.

Krogstad   I'll wait for you downstairs.

Kristine   Will you?

Krogstad   Of course I will.

Kristine   You could walk me back to my lodgings.

Krogstad   I can't quite believe this is happening to me.

He leaves.
She watches him go.
She thinks.
She smiles deeply.
She tidies up a little. She picks up her outdoor clothes.
She listens.
She puts on her hat and coat.
Torvald *and* **Nora** *come into the hall from the outside.*
Nora *is dressed in her gypsy costume.*
Torvald *is wearing a dinner jacket.*

Nora   No. No. No. I'm not coming. I'm not, Torvald. I'm
going back upstairs. It's too early.

Torvald   Nora.

Nora   Oh please, Torvald. Don't be boring. I'll ask in my
nicest voice. I'll sing for you. I'll do anything you want me to
do, Torvald. Just one more hour.

Torvald   Not one more minute. My beautiful, sweet Nora.
We made a deal. You promised me. Now. Go into the drawing
room. You'll catch a cold standing out here.

He leads her into the drawing room.

Kristine   Good evening.

Nora   Kristine!

Torvald   Mrs Linde. What on earth are you doing here?

Kristine   I'm so sorry Mr Helmer. I so wanted to see Nora's
costume.

Nora   Have you been sitting here all this time waiting for me?

Kristine   I have, I'm afraid. I was rather late. You'd gone
by the time I got here but I didn't think I could leave until I'd
seen you.

Torvald *takes* **Nora***'s shawl off her shoulders.*

Torvald   You were right to wait, Mrs Linde. Doesn't she
look breathtaking?

Kristine   Yes. I think she –

Torvald   Doesn't she look absolutely breathtaking? Everybody
said so. At the party. But she is, I have to tell you, Mrs Linde,
terribly strong willed. This creature. What should we do with
her? Do you know, I almost had to force her to leave?

Nora   Well, Torvald. You'll regret you didn't let me stay.

Torvald   Mrs Linde, can you hear the way she speaks to me?
She dances the tarantella. She's a triumph. Although her
performance was a little too natural, for my taste. A little bit

too free with the strictures of the art form, you understand. But we can forgive that! The point is: she's a triumph. A real triumph. Now. Should I let her loiter after that? That would diminish the effect, Mrs Linde, don't you agree? No, thank you very much. I took the arm of my beautiful gypsy girl from Capri; capricious Capri you could say couldn't you? My little capricious Capri. One swift round through the room. And my beautiful girl, as they say in the novels, disappeared into thin air.

I always think an exit should be dramatic. Don't you, Mrs Linde? But Nora here just doesn't get that. She doesn't understand it at all. Good Lord, it's hot in here.

He throws his dinner jacket on to a chair and opens the door to his study.

My God. It's pitch black in there. Oh yes. Silly me.
Excuse me.

He goes into his office to light some of the candles.
Nora *looks to* **Kristine**.

Kristine   I've spoken to him.

Nora   What did he say?

Kristine   Nora, you must tell Torvald everything.

Nora*'s face falls.*

Kristine   You have nothing to be afraid of. Not from Krogstad. But you have to tell him. He's your husband.

Nora   I'm not saying a word.

Kristine   Before he reads the letter.

Beat.
Nora *looks at* **Kristine**.

Nora   Yes. Thank you, Kristine. I know what I need to do. Shhh.

Torvald *comes back.*

Torvald   So. Mrs Linde. Have you had a chance to admire her in all her glory?

Kristine   I have, Mr Helmer, thank you. And now I must say good night.

Torvald   So soon? Is this your knitting?

Kristine   Yes. Thank you. I almost forgot it.

Torvald   So. You knit do you? A bit of a knitter?

Kristine   Yes. I'm afraid I am.

Torvald   You should do embroidery instead really.

Kristine   And why's that?

Torvald   It's just. It's far more beautiful, don't you think? Look. I'll show you. You hold, when you do embroidery, when you're embroidering, you, you, you hold the embroidery here with your left hand. Like this. And then you guide the needle through with your right hand like this. In. Out. In. Out.

He pauses to check the women are watching him. Then carries on.

In. Out. In. Out. In. Out. In. Out. Little light movements. It's good, isn't it?

Kristine   Yes. I suppose it is.

Torvald   But knitting. It's just bloody ugly. Look. Your arms are all squashed up. The knitting needles going up and down. Up and down. There's something Chinese about it.

God, that was good champagne.

Kristine   Well. Goodnight. Goodnight, Nora. And really, Mr Helmer is right. You shouldn't be so wilful any more.

Torvald   Thank you, Mrs Linde. Well said, that woman!

Kristine   Goodnight.

He accompanies her into the hall and out of the apartment.

Torvald   Goodnight. Goodnight, my dear. Will you get home safely? I'd offer to walk you home but it's not far really, is it?

Kristine   Not at all. Goodnight.

Torvald   Goodnight. Goodnight then.

She leaves the apartment.

Off you go.

He comes back in.

God, she's boring. I thought she'd never leave.

Nora   Are you a little bit tired, my love?

Torvald   Not in any way.

Nora   Not just a little bit sleepy?

Torvald   Not in the least. Quite the contrary. I feel incredibly awake. Don't you?

Nora *yawns. Tries to cover it.*

Nora   I'm sorry.

Torvald   You see. I was right to take you home with me.

Nora   You're always right. You always know what's best for me.

She goes to him. She rests herself against him.

Torvald   My swallow's back.

He tries to kiss her.
She lets him kiss her head. Then she backs away from him.

Did you notice?

Nora   What?

Torvald   How cheerful Dr Rank was this evening?

Nora   I didn't really get a chance to talk to him.

Torvald   No. I didn't either really. But I was watching him. I've not seen him in such a good mood for a very long time. He was positively jolly.

He looks at her for a while. He moves to her.

It's so good to be home. With you. Alone. My beautiful, precious –

Nora   Don't.

Torvald   ?

Nora   Look at me like that.

Torvald   I'm sorry?

Nora   Please, Torvald I'm –

Torvald   Why not? You're my most treasured possession. You're so beautiful. You're mine.

She moves away from him.

Nora   Don't, Torvald.

He follows her.

Torvald   Don't what?

He holds her.

You still have the tarantella coursing through your blood. Don't you? I can sense it. It makes me want you even more. God, you smell so good. Shhh. Listen. All the guests are starting to leave. Soon this whole place will be silent.

Nora   I hope so.

Torvald   It'll be as though we've got the whole building to ourselves. When I'm at a party with you. Do you know why I hardly speak to you? Do you know why I keep myself so far away from you? I just glance at you? I steal glances. From time to time. Do you know why I do that? It's because, in my head, I'm imagining that you are my secret lover. My young, secret lover and nobody knows that there is anything between us at all.

Nora *smiles at him.*

Torvald   And then, when it's time to go. And I wrap your shawl around your beautiful, young shoulders, around the wonderful curve of your neck. Then. I imagine that you are my young bride and we have only just been married that night and I am taking you to my home for the first time. That I will be alone with you for the first time. Quite alone. With you and your young – Trembling. When I saw you chase and tempt in the tarantella. I was on fire. I could hardly stand it. That was why I had to take you home with me.

Nora   Get off me. Torvald, I don't want this.

Torvald   What?

Are you teasing me? Are you playing with me, little one? I'm your husband.

A knock is heard on the front door.
They stare at one another.

Torvald *calls.*

Torvald   Who is it?

Rank   It's only me. Can I come in, just for a moment?

Torvald *sits on his fury.*

Torvald   Just coming.

He goes to let him in.

Rank   I thought I heard your voices as I was passing, and I thought I would pop in. I was quite sure you wouldn't want me to just walk past your door and leave you alone for a peaceful evening without being pestered by your friends.

Torvald   Absolutely not, of course we wouldn't, my dear Doctor.

Rank *comes into the room.*

Rank   It's so warm in here. And cosy. And jolly.

Torvald   You've been having a jolly night all night really, haven't you, Dr Rank?

Rank   You're right. I have. And why not? One should try everything in this world. At least once. I thought I'd see what jollity felt like.

The wine, tonight, was just splendid –

Torvald   The champagne especially.

Rank   Beautifully dry. *Méthode champenoise*. It is almost incredible how much of it I managed to wash down.

Nora   Almost as much as Torvald, I'm sure.

Rank   Is that right?

Nora   And now he's really a little bit drunk.

Rank   Well, why not? Why shouldn't a man enjoy himself after a hard day's work?

Torvald   I wish I had that excuse, Dr Rank!

Rank   Don't you?

Torvald   Not today.

Rank *slaps his back.*

Rank   I do!

Nora   Dr Rank. I believe you have carried out a scientific experiment today.

Rank   I have. Precisely. I have.

Torvald   Listen to her! 'Scientific experiments!'

Nora   And would I be right to congratulate you on the result?

Rank   I dare say you could.

Nora   Was it what you hoped it would be?

Rank   It was the best possible result. For doctor and patient alike. Certainty.

Nora   Certainty?

Rank   Absolute certainty. So. I think I deserve a jolly evening, a little celebration, after a result like that, don't you?

Nora   Of course you do, Dr Rank.

Torvald   Just so long as you don't suffer too much tomorrow.

Rank   There is no such thing as an action without consequence in this life, Mr Helmer old chap.

Nora   Dr Rank, I believe you are keen on these fancy dress parties, are you not?

Rank   Oh, indeed I am. As long as there are plenty of wonderful fanciful costumes and lots of −

Nora   What shall we two dress as at the next one?

Torvald   You cheeky little playful little − are you already thinking about −

Rank   Us two?

Nora   Yes. Us two.

Rank   Well. I'll tell you. You shall be the child of fortune.

Torvald   Well, that's a brilliant idea. Good luck finding a costume for that!

Rank   Oh, Torvald. She would only need to appear exactly as she is. She could walk through the party exactly as she walks through this world.

Torvald   Ha! Very good! Very clever!

Nora   And do you know what you're going to be?

Rank   Yes. Do you know, Nora, I am absolutely sure of it.

Torvald   Oh yes?

Rank   At the next costume ball I shall be invisible.

Torvald   What an odd idea.

Rank   There is a big, black hat, have you never heard of it? Have you never heard of the big, black hat of invisibility? What you do with this hat is, you put it on and then no one can see you at all.

Torvald   That sounds extraordinary.

Rank   But I'm completely forgetting what I came here for. Helmer. Give me a cigar. One of the dark Havanas.

Torvald   With pleasure.

He offers him the box.

Rank *takes one and cuts the end off it.*

Rank   Thank you. It's all I came for, really.

He goes to light it but before he can do so **Nora** *strikes a light.*

Nora   Let me light it.

Rank   Thank you Nora.

He bends to her. She lights his cigar.

So.

He smokes.

Goodbye, Mr and Mrs Helmer.

Torvald   Goodbye, my friend.

Nora   Sleep well, Dr Rank.

Rank   Thank you. I will, Nora. Thank you for that.

Nora   Wish me the same.

Rank   You? Oh. If I must. Sleep well, Nora.
And thank you. For the cigar. And for the light.

He nods to them both.
He leaves.

Torvald *takes out his keys and goes to the hall.*

Nora   Where are you going?

Torvald (*off*)   I have to empty the post box. It's completely full up. There won't be room for the papers tomorrow.

Nora   Are you working tonight?

Torvald (*off*)   I don't want to. You know very well I don't want to.

Someone's been at the lock.

Nora   The lock?

Torvald (*off*)   Somebody's been trying to open it. There's a, a, a broken hairpin lodged in it. It's one of yours.

Nora   It must have been one of the children.

Torvald (*off*)   You really must tell them not to do that again. Hm. Hm. Got it.

Helene! Put the light out in the hall. For goodness' sake. That girl.

He enters. He has a pile of letters in his hand.

Look. Two days' post. It's ridiculous.

He leafs through the pile. He stops.

What's this?

Nora *heads to the window. She can barely watch.*

Torvald   Two visiting cards.

Nora *turns.*

Nora   From Doctor Rank?

Torvald   Rank. Doctor of Medicine. They were on the top of the pile. He must have posted them as he was leaving.

Nora   Do they say anything?

Torvald   Nothing. There's a black cross over his name. Here, look. What a horrible idea. It's like he's announcing his own death.

Nora   He is.

Torvald   What do you mean, he is? What are you talking about, 'he is'?

She looks at him. Holds his gaze.

What has he told you?

Nora   He said that when he leaves two calling cards marked with a black cross in our post box then that is his way of saying goodbye to us both. His illness has become incurable. He's decided to shut himself away and die.

It takes **Torvald** *a time to make sense of this.*

Torvald   My poor friend. I knew I wouldn't get to keep him long. But so soon – To hide himself away like a wounded animal.

Nora   Maybe it's better that these things happen without words, Torvald.

Torvald   He can't just – He's part of us, Nora. I can't imagine him not being here. With his grumpiness and his suffering and his loneliness.

He smokes.

Maybe it's better this way. For him. Maybe for us too, Nora.

Now we are quite dependent on one another.

He goes to her.
He holds her.

My beautiful, beloved wife. Sometimes I don't think I can possibly hold you tight enough. Can I confess something to you, Nora? Sometimes I have fantasies about you being threatened by a terrible danger just so that I can risk my life and everything, risk everything for your sake.

She breaks free of him.

Nora   Read your letters, Torvald.

Torvald   No. Not tonight. Tonight I want to be with you, my beautiful, beloved wife.

Nora   While we think of your friend, dying?

Torvald   Yes. You're right. It's upset everything hasn't it? Ugliness has appeared. Thoughts of death and of destruction. We have to shake them out of our heads. Maybe we should go to our own rooms?

She puts her arms around his neck.

Nora   I think I need to, Torvald. I'm so sorry.

Torvald   You mustn't be.

Nora   I know. It's just – I'm so tired.

He kisses her forehead.

Torvald   Goodnight. Little bird. Sleep well. My love. My
Nora. You go to sleep. I'll read my letters. I will see you in the
morning.

He kisses her.
He takes the letters into his study.

She stumbles.
She sits down.
She fumbles around.
She finds his jacket.
She throws it around herself.
She waits.
Torvald *opens his study door.*
He has an open letter in his hand.

Nora.

She gasps. Cowers away from him.

You know. Don't you? What's written in this letter.

Nora   Let me go. Let me go, please.

Torvald   Where are you going?

Nora   Please don't try and stop me. Please let me go, Torvald.

Torvald   Is it true, what he's written?

Nora   I have loved you more than anything in the world.

Torvald   Is that meant to be some kind of excuse?

You miserable –

Nora   Let me go. Let me out.

Torvald   Shut up. You're not going anywhere.

He locks the door.

Do you realise what you've done?

Answer me.

Do you realise what you've done?

Nora   I think I do. I think I'm starting to.

Torvald   Horrible.

After all these years.

She was. I really thought she was. Do you know? I thought she was my pride and joy?

Hyprocrite. Liar.

She stares at him.

I should have known. Her father's daughter.

Be quiet!

No religion. No morality. No sense of duty. Everything he lacked she lacks too! Everything he did she does too. Of course she does.

Everything I did for him I did for your sake and this is how you reward me?

Nora   Yes. It is.

Torvald   You have ruined my happiness. You have ruined my future.

Terrible.

He can do whatever he wants with me now. He can ask whatever he wants.

Nora   When I'm dead he won't be able to do a –

Torvald   Oh, don't be so pathetic. You sound exactly like your father. How would it help me if you were dead? What difference would that make? None. Everybody will think that it was my idea. They'll think I encouraged you. Do you have the slightest idea what you've done to me?

Nora   Yes. I do.

Torvald   Take off my jacket. Take it off.

I'll contact him. I'll give him what he wants.

You're going nowhere. You're staying here in my house. Everything is staying exactly as it was before. You're never seeing the children again. I can't trust you with them. That goes without saying.

I loved you so much. That stops. From this moment on I am simply concerned with saving the remains. The pieces.

The doorbell goes.

Is this him? Has he – ? Get out. Go and hide. You're sick. We'll tell him that's where you are.

She doesn't move.
Helene *enters.*
She is dressed for bed with a coat over her night things.
She is very tired.

Helene   A letter arrived for you, ma'am.

Torvald   Give it to me. Now go.

Helene *goes.*

Torvald   You're not having it. It's from him.

He opens the letter.
He holds it to a light.
He reads it.
He looks at an enclosed piece of paper.
Nora *watches him.*
He gasps for breath.
She goes to take the letter.
He won't give it to her.

Torvald   I need to read it again.

He reads it again.
He looks at her.
He smiles.

Nora   What does it say?

He looks at her.
His smile turns into a laugh.

He passes her the letter.
He laughs loudly and almost hysterically.
At times it is like he is laughing in her face.

Torvald   I'm saved. And you. Of course. Both of us. We're saved. 'I am returning your contract of debt with immediate effect. I regret and repent all of the misery I have caused you since Christmas Eve.' How does it go? 'A' – a what? – 'A fortunate event in my life –' A what? A fortunate event in his life?! We are saved, Nora. By a fortunate event in his life. Here. Give it to me.

He takes the letter and the contract and tears them into hundreds of pieces and throws them on the fire.
He is still laughing.
He's maniacal.

Since Christmas Eve? You must have had a terrible few days, Nora?!

Nora   It's been horrible.

Torvald   You must have, you must have, have, have tortured yourself. I bet you couldn't see any other way out other than to – No. Let's not think about that. It's over. It's over. It's over. It's over. It's over.

What's the matter?

Nora, what's the matter? Your face. You look frozen.

Oh. I see. You can't believe that I've forgiven you everything.

I have.

I have, you know. Everything you did, you did out of love for me.

Nora   That's true.

Torvald   And you were right to. You were right to, Nora. You just didn't quite understand what it actually involved. Did you? Do you think I love you any less because you don't have the slightest idea how to act on your own?

No. Nora. You can always rely on me. You can always lean on me. I will always advise you.

Can I confess something to you? I actually find your lack of
insight and lack of understanding and lack of ability to know
what to do rather attractive. It makes me realise that I am a
man and you are a woman.

Are you cross with me? Are you cross with me because of
the things that I said? Don't be. I promise you, Nora. I've
forgiven you.

Nora   Thank you.

She goes to head back to her room.

Torvald   Where are you going?

Nora   To take my costume off.

Torvald   Yes. Do that. Calm yourself down. Get your
thoughts together. My frightened little skylark. I'll watch over
you. You're a hunted dove I have saved from the hawk's claws.

She leaves into her room.

Keep your door open. I want to talk to you.

She does.

It will happen, Nora.

Tomorrow everything will look quite different to you. Soon
I won't even have to tell you any more that I've forgiven you.
You'll feel it. It will feel so certain.

Can I confess something else to you? It feels so sweet. It feels
so satisfying to forgive my wife. It's like you have become mine
all over again. Only twice as strongly as before. In a way it's
like I've given you a new life. In a way it's a little bit like you're
my wife and you've also now become my child. That's how it is.
From this point on.

You don't need to be afraid of anything any more.

She comes back out.
She is in her day clothes.

What are you doing? I thought you were going to sleep. Have
you not got changed?

Nora   I am changed, Torvald.

Torvald   What are you talking about, it's late, Nora.

Nora   I'm not going to sleep tonight.

Torvald   What do you mean, you're not –

Nora   It's not that late.

Sit down, Torvald.

She sits at one side of the table.

Torvald   Why are you looking at me like that?

Nora   You should sit down, Torvald. There's rather a lot
I want to say.

He looks at her for a time.
He sits down.

Torvald   I'm not sure I understand what you're –

Nora   No. You don't. You don't understand me at all. And
I don't think I've ever understood you. Until now. Until
tonight. Don't interrupt me.

Just. Listen.

Do you notice anything odd about the way we're sitting?

Torvald   The way we're –

Nora   The way we're sitting here.

Torvald   I'm not sure. What do you –

Nora   We've been married for nine years. This is the first
time that you and I have had a serious discussion.

Torvald   What do you mean, 'serious'?

Nora   Even before we got married. We've never exchanged
a serious word about anything.

He looks at her for a time.

Torvald   I'm rather confused, Nora, I have to confess. Are
you refusing to sleep tonight because you've suddenly realised

that you always wanted me to share all my worries with you? I'm afraid I don't really see the point of that. You couldn't have helped me deal with any of them –

Nora   Not worries. I'm not talking about sharing worries. I'm talking about sitting down and seriously trying to make sense of things. To understand things.

Torvald   Nora, are you saying that you would have preferred it if we did that?

Nora   You don't understand, do you? You never have. I've been terribly treated, Torvald. First by my father and then by you.

Torvald   What?

A very long pause. He struggles to understand this idea.

We are the two people who loved you more than –

Nora   You didn't. You never loved me. You just enjoyed the idea of being in love with me.

What? It's true.

When I was growing up my father told me all his opinions and so I inherited those opinions and if I ever had any other opinions then I hid them from him because they would have made him furious. He called me his doll. He played with me like I used to play with my dolls. Then I was taken to your house.

Torvald   What kind of expression is that?

Nora   An accurate one. You took me from my father's house to yours. And the same thing happened here. You furnished according to your taste. So I developed the same taste as you. Or I pretended to. I'm not sure. Maybe it was both. I've lived my whole marriage like a beggar. Like a street entertainer. I survive by performing tricks for you. That's how you like it. It's your fault and my father's fault that I've never made anything of myself.

A long pause.

He laughs a bit.
Then stops.

Torvald   Are you trying to tell me that you've never been happy here?

Nora   Never. Not happy.

Torvald   You ungrateful, unreasonable –

Nora   I've been cheerful. That's not the same. You've always been very kind to me. But none of this was real, you know? This wasn't really a house. It was a playroom. I've been your doll. Just as I was my father's doll when I was a little girl. And the children have become my dolls. I thought it was fun when you played with me. They thought it was fun when I played with them. None of it was real in any way.

Torvald   So maybe it should be different now. Is that what you're suggesting? Maybe playtime's over now. Maybe now it's time for learning.

Nora   Who needs to learn, Torvald? Me or the children?

Torvald   Both you and the children.

Nora   Oh my love. You can't teach me anything.

Torvald   I could –

Nora   I can't teach the children anything either. You said so yourself. You couldn't trust me with them.

Torvald   I was angry.

Nora   You were right. There's something I need to do before I try and teach anybody anything.

She looks at him for a time.

I need to teach myself. You can't do it. I've got to do it on my own. That's why I'm leaving you.

Torvald   You're what?

Nora   I can't live with you any longer.

Torvald   Nora.

Nora   I have to stand up on my own.

Kristine can put me up for the night.

Torvald   This is mad. I won't let you.

Nora   You can't stop me. I'll take all my things.
I won't take anything from you. Either now or later.

Torvald   You're insane.

Nora   Tomorrow I'll go back home. To where I came from.
It will be easier for me to find something to do there.

Torvald   You have no idea what would happen to you.

Nora   No. Of course I don't. I can't possibly have any idea
until I've done it.

Torvald   This is your home. You can't leave your husband.
You can't leave your children.

Nora   Why not?

Torvald   What will people say about you?

Nora   I don't care about that.

Torvald   This is monstrous. You have responsibilities. You
can't just abandon –

Nora   What responsibilities?

Torvald   Responsibilities to your husband. Responsibilities
to your children.

Nora   What about my responsibilities to myself?

Torvald   You are a wife and a mother. Before anything else.

Nora   I think I'm a human being before anything else. I
don't care what other people say. I don't care what people
write in books. I need to think for myself.

Torvald   What you're suggesting goes against every religious
tenet –

Nora   I don't even know what religion really is any more.

All I remember is what Pastor Hansen told me when I was confirmed. He said that religion meant this. And that religion meant that. He said Jesus meant this and that Jesus meant that. I need to get away from here and be on my own for a while so I can see with clarity if what he said was right.

Torvald   What you're suggesting is immoral. Can't you feel that? In your, in your, in your soul.

Nora   I don't know. I don't even know if I have a soul or if anybody has a soul or if there's any such thing as a soul. There has to be doesn't there? I just don't know if there is. All I know is that I have a different opinion on this matter than you do. I thought I knew what the law was. I was wrong. I didn't realise that it was against the law for a woman to spare her old, dying father or to save her husband's life. I didn't realise that.

Torvald   You're talking like a child. You don't understand, do you? You don't understand religion or morality or responsibility or society. You don't understand the society you live in.

Nora   I don't even really know what society is. I don't know if there's any such thing.

Torvald   You're ill. You're going out of your mind.

Nora   I'm not. I've never felt so clear. I've never felt so certain.

Torvald   You're going to leave your husband? You're going to leave your children?

Nora *nods.*

Torvald   So.

Nora   What?

Torvald   You don't love me any more.

Nora   No. I don't think I do.

Torvald   How can you say that to me?

Nora   I don't know. It hurts me to say it. You've always been so kind to me. But I can't help it. I don't love you any more. I can't live here any more.

Torvald   I don't understand. Can you explain to me? How did this happen? What did I do wrong?

Nora   It was tonight. I was waiting for a miracle to happen. It didn't. That's when I realised. You're not the man I hoped you were.

Torvald   I don't know what you're talking about.

Nora   I've been waiting for it for so long. I know that miracles don't happen every day. I waited for nine years for mine. And then after Christmas Eve, since Krogstad first told me what he'd figured out, I knew then, I was completely certain, that it was time for my miracle to happen. And then his letter was out there. And I never thought for a second you would do what he told you. I was so certain you would stand up to him. I was certain you would tell him to go and reveal everything to the world. And then –

Torvald   Yes, what would you do then? After I'd exposed you to shame and humiliation?

Nora   Then I thought with unshakeable faith and certainty that you would step forward and take the blame and tell the world that it was you. That you were guilty.

Torvald   Nora –

Nora   I would have denied it, of course. Nobody would have believed me. That was the miracle I was waiting for. I was ready to end my life to stop you from doing it.

Torvald   I would have done anything for you. I would have worked day and night. I would have put up with anything for you. But no man would sacrifice his, his, his honour. Even for the person he loves.

Nora   Thousands and thousands and thousands of women have done.

Torvald   You're not thinking. You're talking like a child.

Nora   Maybe. But you're not talking or thinking like a man I can spend my life with. When you calmed down, when you realised you were no longer in danger you seemed to think that nothing had happened. You thought I could be your skylark again. Your doll. You thought I was weak. You thought I was fragile. You told me I was your child. I knew then that for nine years I had lived with a stranger and that I had had three children with – Oh. I can't bear to think about it. I could tear myself to pieces.

Torvald   I can see that. I understand. I've done something I never intended to do. And because of what I did there is a gulf between us. But Nora, can't we close it?

Nora   Not any more. I am not your wife any more.

Torvald   I can change. I can find the strength to become another man.

Nora   Maybe. If your doll is taken away from you.

Torvald   I can't imagine being apart from you.

Nora   That's exactly why I need to go.

She stands.
She goes to her room.
She returns with her coat and a small bag.
She puts the bag down on the chair by the table.

Torvald   Nora. Not now. Wait until tomorrow.

She puts her coat on.

Nora   I can't. I can't spend the night in a stranger's house.

Torvald   Can't we? Can't we? Can't we live here? Like brother and sister?

Nora   You know that wouldn't last long. It couldn't.

She wraps the shawl about herself.

I won't see the little ones. They're in better hands than mine. The way I am now. I would be nothing to them.

Torvald   Maybe not now. But one day –

Nora   I don't know. I don't even know what will happen to me.

Torvald   You're my wife. You always will be.

Nora   Torvald. When a wife leave's a husband's house.
According to all law he is released from any obligations
towards her. I release you of all obligations to me. You're
bound by nothing. There is total freedom on both sides.

She takes her ring off.

Look.

She puts it on the table in front of him.

Here is your ring. Give me mine.

Torvald   Your ring?

She nods.
He takes his ring off.
He gives it to her.

Nora   There. Now. It's over. I will leave my keys here.
Helene knows more about the house than I do. Anna knows
more about the children. Tomorrow Kristine will come here
to pack the things that I brought with me from home. She can
send them to me.

I will think of you often, Torvald. And of the children. And of
this house. You must never write to me. You must send me
nothing. I can't take any help from you. People shouldn't take
help from strangers.

Torvald   Nora. Can I never be more than a stranger to you?

Nora   The most wonderful thing would have to happen first.
A miracle.

Torvald   What miracle?

Nora   You and I would both have to change so much that –

Torvald, I don't believe in miracles any more.

Torvald   But I do. Tell me. We'd have to change so much
that − ?

She smiles at him.

Nora   Goodbye, Torvald.

She exits through the hall.
Torvald *listens.*
She closes the front door.
He waits.
He sits. He buries his face in his hands.
He thinks he hears her.

Torvald   Nora.

He looks up. He goes to the door.
The door to the street is slammed downstairs.